the
DIVERSITY
TRAINING
handbook

A PRACTICAL GUIDE TO UNDERSTANDING
& CHANGING ATTITUDES

2nd edition

PHIL CLEMENTS & JOHN JONES

**KOGAN
PAGE**

London and Philadelphia

First published in 2002
Second edition 2006
Reprinted 2007

Kogan Page Limited
120 Pentonville Road
London N1 9JN
UK
www.kogan-page.co.uk

Kogan Page US
525 South 4th Street, #241
Philadelphia PA 19147
USA

© Phil Clements and John Jones, 2002, 2006

ISBN-10:   0 7494 4476 2
ISBN-13:   978 0 7494 4476 1

British Library Cataloguing in Publication Data

A CIP record for this book is available from the British Library.

Library of Congress Cataloging-in-Publication Data

Clements, Phillip Edward.
    The diversity training handbook : a practical guide to understanding and changing attitudes / Phil Clements and John Jones.—2nd ed.
        p. cm.
    ISBN 0-7494-4476-2
    1. Diversity in the workplace. 2. Employees—Training of. 3. Attitude change. 4. Discrimination in employment. I. Jones, John, 1960– II. Title.
HF5549.5.M5C586 2006
658.3008—dc22

                              2005026527

Typeset by JS Typesetting Ltd, Porthcawl, Mid Glamorgan
Printed and bound in Great Britain by Cambrian Printers Ltd, Aberystwyth, Wales

Contents

Acknowledgements

My thinking about diversity has been and still is developing partly as a result of formal research, partly from self-reflection, but most of all from the influence of others whose diverse perspectives and world-views have all in their way been formative of my own.

My sincere thanks to the individuals who have made me 'pause for reflection' in the same way we hope you will as you read the book. These people include Angela Morrell, Christine Marriott, Sandra Johnson, Tom Kelly, Wycliffe Barrett, Inder Singh Uppal, Keith Wood, Alistair Seddon, Jaslien Singh, Manny Barot, Fran Richley, Deepak Mahtani, Morcea Walker, Harold Mangar, Tim Meaklim, Bruce Campion-Smith, Richard Martin, Hugh Dent, Charles Carrington, and many others including all the learners I have had the privilege of working (and learning) with over the years.

Thanks to my sons Tom and Matthew, who, as they have progressed through university, have become ever more challenging.

But most of all I sincerely thank Heather, my wife, constant support and best friend, for putting up with my self-indulgent need to write.

Phil Clements

There have been a number of people who have helped me along my own particular journey of discovery and development and it is impossible to thank, or indeed name, them all. Much of my own development is the result of unplanned conversations and discussions, observations and giving myself the time to reflect on the journey to date.

Heartfelt thanks must go to those people that have trusted my ability to continue the journey and given me the inspiration to travel further. This group includes, but is not limited to, Tom Williamson, Steve Savage, Jerome Mack, Dianna Yach, Peter Hermitage, Ann Ashworth, Richard Griggs, Tony

Spinks, Shafiq Mogul and more recently Philip Rowbourne, Peter Millard and Kathie Gilley.

Thanks also to my good friend and co-author, who continues to be a constant source of knowledge, energy, and enthusiasm.

To family and friends who have supported me throughout this venture I will try in some way to repay the investment you have made in me.

In particular thanks must go to my daughter Amie and son Matthew, two very special people, who have deserved a lot more of my attention during the past year.

To Lesley, I know that these few words can never repay your support, trust, commitment and love. Thank you for being there, it would never have been possible without you.

My contribution to this project is dedicated to my late father, Chas.

John Jones

Chapter 1

Approaching Diversity

By the time you have worked through this opening chapter we hope that you will have:

- gained an appreciation of who we are and our expectations of who you might be;
- acquired an understanding of what assumptions we are making as we write the book;
- considered why managing diversity and diversity training might be called 'special' and warrant such detailed consideration;
- reflected on the various roles that it is useful to identify in managing the change that diversity often implies;
- been challenged by the profile of a diversity trainer/manager and considered the skills and attributes that such a person needs;
- reflected on meeting the challenge of self-development;
- acquired an understanding of how we have written the book and how we hope you will use it.

WHO WE ARE; WHO YOU ARE

We want to state quite clearly at the outset that this book is about the concept and outworking of diversity. It is not about the diverse communities that exist in Britain today. As we shall see as the argument unfolds, it would be quite wrong for us to purport to speak on behalf of others. Not only are they quite capable of doing that for themselves, the very notion of two white heterosexual males speaking on behalf of others who view the world differently would be alien to a proper understanding of diversity. What we can and do want to do is present the arguments for diversity and discuss some of the underpinning concepts and knowledge. In doing so we will draw on many years of experience of working in the field of understanding and changing attitudes and behaviour, with both large organizations and small groups.

Those years have seen many changes in emphasis. In the 1980s we were working in community and race relations (CRR). This gave way to a more generalized approach which encompassed the broader issues subsumed in the label 'equal opportunities'. Following the publication in 1999 of the Macpherson Report on *The Stephen Lawrence Inquiry*, the focus shifted back to CRR. There were a number of initiatives in the police and criminal justice system, among others, that addressed issues of race equality, particularly institutional racism. This has not unnaturally led to a groundswell of opinion that in fact, while not losing sight of the fact that in Britain today there are still enormous problems of racial inequality, many diverse groups face similar problems of disadvantage and discrimination. This brings us to consider who you are.

Of course we can have no real idea of who you are, but the very fact that you are reading this suggests that for some reason you are interested in diversity. In fact we hope that you may be more than interested. We hope that you want to consider the issues, perhaps in more depth than you have up till now, with a view to embracing and celebrating diversity more fully. In our view, to embrace diversity is to come to a position of belief that the ways in which we all differ:

- are a reality that should not and must not be ignored;
- do not equal 'difficult' and 'problem';
- mean that we can accept that people see the world differently and that those world-views have equal validity;
- are not threatening;
- are positive things rather than negative;
- are to be inclusive rather than exclusive;
- are likely to involve some personal change.

Likewise we believe that to celebrate diversity is:

- to enjoy the friendship and support of people from backgrounds different from ourselves;
- to explore and enjoy the rich variety of culture that a diverse population offers;

- to do all we can to ensure people are treated as individuals, fairly and with dignity and respect;
- a self-developmental exercise in which we become more rounded, less insular people;
- something to live rather than merely to discuss.

You might well be a leader in your own organization or in what you do. This does not necessarily mean that you will be 'high up' in the management or command structure. It is our frequent experience that many true leaders in organizations come from lower down in the management structures. These are people who through their dedication and commitment become agents for change in their organization. If you are a leader who is in a position to influence or direct strategy and policy, then you have an even greater responsibility to address and lead on diversity. We feel sure that this book will give you some insight into ways in which you might achieve just that.

We are writing not only with managers and leaders in mind but also trainers and educators. If you are involved in training or education around diversity issues, you will not need us to tell you how demanding this can be. We hope that this book will contribute to your toolkit of skills and knowledge to help you do your job that little bit easier. Before moving on, have a go at the 'diversity health check' in Figure 1.1. It is neither a scientific instrument, nor a comprehensive self-diagnosis, but it will steer you towards some common issues in diversity and our approach to it that may be revealing.

It is not our intention to go into detail about how you might have answered the questions. To a large extent that is a matter for you, and only you will know what your position is on the issues. Having said that, we can make some broader observations:

- Do you know what diversity is?
- How much does the exercise reveal what you know about how much you know about yourself? Were you able to identify your values? Could you be honest with yourself about your prejudices?
- How much do you know about the law relating to diversity?
- Do you have a sound understanding of institutional racism and discrimination? Are you able to relate this to how the phenomenon manifests itself in organizations?

To put all this more simply, to fully appreciate diversity we all need to develop a good understanding of ourselves, the way we see the world, and

What do you understand diversity to be?	
What are your nine most treasured values?	
If someone asked you what were your prejudices – what would you say? What would you say you were doing to manage them?	
What diversities do you recognize in: • society at large? • the organization or company you work for?	
Are you able to explain and give examples of: • institutional racism? • institutional discrimination?	
Think about when you discuss diversity issues with people, and give some examples of what issues make you feel defensive.	
Make a note of the main legislation in the UK that deals with discrimination.	
What is the European Convention on Human Rights?	
Give some examples of how you promote diversity in your interactions with others.	
What communities do you identify with?	
Give examples of how you are demonstrating leadership in support of diversity.	

Figure 1.1   *Diversity health check*

the way others may see the world. This needs to be grounded in the contexts in which all this takes place, namely society at large and more specifically the organizations and institutions in which we live and work.

ASSUMPTIONS

In several places in the text, we will be referring to the danger of making assumptions. This includes making assumptions about whiteness, making assumptions about groups we may have labelled or stereotyped, and making assumptions that others will view the world in the same way as we do. So in order to practise what we preach we need to be explicit about the assumptions we are both making and not making as we unfold our approach to diversity.

- We are assuming that you are reading this text with an open mind and that you will consider carefully what you are reading.
- We are assuming that you will engage in the exercises in the book.
- We are not making the assumption that we have a monopoly on the truth about diversity. Rather we are opening up the issues as we see them and fully recognize that others may see them differently.
- We are assuming that since you have already expressed an interest in diversity, you will follow up by finding out more about the diverse communities that make up society in Britain. We have already noted that it is not our intention to present much information about diverse communities themselves. That is best left for you to find out first-hand.

DIVERSITY AND DIVERSITY TRAINING AS A 'SPECIAL' CASE

In what ways can diversity be seen as a special case? Why is there a need for a handbook on diversity at all? We noted above that in some ways diversity can be seen as having evolved out of equal opportunities and community and race relations. As such the body of knowledge about, and approaches to, diversity are not nearly as accessible as is, say, the literature on equal opportunities. Of course diversity is not new in itself, but the groundswell of thinking about it most certainly is. We want to suggest a number of reasons why diversity can be considered special.

- There is an increasing recognition that embracing diversity is not only a morally good thing, but there is also a sound business case for it. Many organizations both in the public and private sectors have yet to engage properly with the business benefits that positively engaging with diversity can bring. Gidomal, Mahtani and Porter (2001: 37) argue for the importance of understanding and engaging with ethnic minority communities in business: 'Business is at the heart of multi-ethnic Britain's future. Community growth and development are largely based on employment. . . . We believe that it is time to cash in the deposit of talent and skill that is in Britain's ethnic communities and do business together for mutual benefit and profit.'

- Institutional racism and institutional discrimination still blight many organizations. There has been a tendency to take the view that, as time has passed since the challenges to organizations made by the Macpherson Report (1999), the heat is now off and the agenda can shift to something else. This drift towards apathy makes it even more imperative that organizations wake up to the dangers that institutional discrimination can bring.
- The Race Relations (Amendment) Act 2000 places a legal duty on many organizations, among other things, to promote good race relations. These organizations will ignore diversity at their peril.
- Embracing and celebrating diversity is more a way of life than a set of policies. It is no good for an organization to have a diversity strategy and/ or policies. Those policies must be turned into day-to-day realities for its people. Very often this will mean engaging in education, training and awareness programmes, and following through with healthy, effective change management programmes.

ROLES IN MANAGING DIVERSITY

We said above that in writing this text we had managers, leaders and trainers in mind. Having said that, we think it is useful to identify a number of specific roles that people – you – may perhaps adopt in an organization that is wanting positively to nurture and celebrate its diversity. Consider the roles listed in Figure 1.2, and check which ones you may adopt from time to time in your personal or work life.

When an organization truly engages with diversity there is a great deal of work to be done. The work will include setting strategy, implementing change management programmes, checking systems and training/education. The roles will need different sets of skills and abilities, but if there is one outstanding attribute that is common to them all we would say it is commitment. In other words, none of the roles in Figure 1.2 will be effective

Assessor	
Coach	
Counsellor	
Educator	
Evaluator	
Facilitator	
Friend	
Guide	
Leader	
Listener	
Manager	
Mentor	
Researcher	
Strategist	
Tactician	
Trainer	

Figure 1.2 *Roles in diversity management and change*

in managing the change needed for an organization to be healthy in its approach to diversity if the people undertaking the roles are not committed. That means, in simple terms, people 'who walk the talk' and 'own the ethos'. People who engage in this because they believe it in their hearts and are not just doing it to 'tick a box'.

Pause for reflection

If you were put on trial for your commitment to diversity, would there be enough evidence to convict you?

THE PROFILE OF A DIVERSITY TRAINER/MANAGER

What makes a good diversity trainer? In some research that one of us conducted (Clements, 2000), a number of trainers explored their experience of the skills and attributes needed by trainers who are effective in helping people to learn diversity. It is not appropriate to get into a debate here about what a 'skill' is or the difference between skills and attributes. In Table 1.1 what trainers called skills and attributes are listed as they came out of the raw data.

Table 1.1   *Skills and attributes of a diversity trainer/manager*

Skills	Attributes
Makes appropriate interventions	Resilience ('take it on the chin')
Facilitation	Belief in what you are doing
Conflict management	Mental agility
Able to ask tough questions	Deep understanding of issues
Flexible	Positive outlook
Able to manage group dynamics	Recognize own limits
Knowledge of law	Been through the process
Able to manage resistance strategies	Sincerity
Knowledge of policy issues	Sensitive to people's needs and concerns
Knowledge of own prejudice	Non-neutral in facilitation
	'Walk the talk'/'Own the ethos'
	Motivation in the subject
	Well trained in diversity

Of course some of these skills and attributes would be needed by any trainer. But there are a number that, it seems to us, are dimensions of diversity training that go beyond what is normally expected of people who train in other areas. For example, resilience does not just mean the ability to go into a class day after day as is expected of most trainers; it also means being resilient to constant negative views and attitudes of people. It means being resilient as a trainer when you may not feel supported by management in what you are doing. Another key attribute – and we have expressed this already – is the imperative for trainers to believe in what they are doing. The manifestation of this will be 'walking the talk'. All trainers should recognize their own limits, but we believe it is particularly important for the diversity trainer to do so. Our belief is grounded in two things. First, trainers who delve into other people's attitudes, values and beliefs when they are not skilled to do so can end up psychologically damaging the person they are trying to help. Second, trainers themselves will be vulnerable to all sorts of negative effects if they regularly go beyond what they are capable of. These effects include loss of self-esteem, loss of confidence and the manifestations of stress. The effects can be amplified if no support system is in place to act as a safety valve.

Pause for reflection

If you engage in diversity training, what are your limits?
What do you dread happening in a session because it will take you out of your depth?
What can you do about this?

THE CHALLENGE OF SELF-DEVELOPMENT

Lifelong learning is a broad concept, rather than a programme in the traditional sense, and aims to develop a 'learning society' in which everyone, in whatever circumstances, routinely expects to learn and upgrade skills throughout life. We all have a great deal to learn about diversity: not only a better understanding of the reality of diversity in society, but also the issues that this raises. Our experience of diversity training has often been that people will come to such training with the view that there is in fact little that they can learn about diversity. More often than not the view is grounded in assumptions about the white majority in this country and supported by a narrow, even blinkered world-view. So there is a challenge to us all to assess what we still have to learn about diversity and to meet that challenge with openness and a willingness to learn.

The challenge to learn about diversity is even stronger because, as we discuss later, learning to learn about diversity can be, and may even have to be, a painful process. It is not a comfortable experience to learn that we have prejudices we need to deal with. It is not comfortable to find that our own view of the world is just one of many, and those other views are equally valid.

Pause for reflection

Do I want to self-develop, regardless of how old I am or how much life experience I think I have?
How prepared am I to be exposed to issues and realities that may make me feel uncomfortable?

> How ready am I to engage with learning that will challenge my attitudes, values, beliefs and prejudices?
>
> Am I prepared to engage in the uncertainty of learning in an area where there often will be no right answer?

If you want to follow up on the notion of lifelong learning generally, a good website is www.lifelonglearning.co.uk/etda/index.htm.

HOW WE HOPE YOU WILL USE THE BOOK

This is not an academic textbook. Of course we have referenced sources where appropriate, and are confident that our approach will withstand academic scrutiny, but essentially we expect that the book will be of practical value to the practitioner, trainer, manager and person who is concerned to play a role in embracing diversity. In each chapter we open with our 'intentions'. Very often we express these in terms of what we 'hope' you will achieve by working through the text. While we do believe in structured and systematic approaches to training and education, we are not behaviourists. This means that our 'hope' that you will achieve certain things by working through the text embodies the notion that we expect you, as the learner, to do the work.

We say 'work through the text' because we believe this is not the sort of book that you will read through without some effort. We have included several opportunities to pause for reflection and some exercises. Please regard these as essential to your understanding of the particular concept in question, and to your own self-development. Challenge yourself through reflection. If you react to something with surprise, anger and disagreement – even outrage! – ask yourself some penetrating questions and try to answer them honestly. Try questions like:

- Why might this be?
- Why did this provoke such a strong reaction in me?
- Would someone from a different background take a different view? Why?
- What does my reaction say about me, and my values and beliefs?
- Is it possible to hold two views about this at the same time?
- How open am I to being challenged and taken out of my 'comfort zone'?

Where appropriate we have given links to resources or information on the world wide web. We would encourage you to follow these up if you can.

Chapter 2

Making the Case for Diversity

LEARNING INTENTIONS

At the end of this chapter we hope that you will have:

- developed an understanding of the term 'diversity';
- considered the relationship between effective management of diversity and organizational performance;
- identified the major legislative drivers for effectively managing diversity in the United Kingdom;
- explored some organizational strategies to develop effective management of diversity;
- noted the impact of globalization with a specific focus on managing diversity.

INTRODUCTION

In Chapter 1 we began to sketch out some of our underlying assumptions and our approach to diversity training. Since you have reached Chapter 2 of this book we assume that you are keen to develop your own knowledge and understanding of what can be a complex area of personal, professional and organizational development. But what do we mean exactly by the term, and why do we feel that it is important to understand why diversity is such a significant issue in the 21st century?

This chapter attempts to provide some answers to such questions. We begin by proposing a definition of diversity (although it is not the purpose of this book to rely heavily on any particular theoretical and empirical analysis of definitions). We then examine some of the drivers that make understanding the nature and practical implications of diversity such a crucial challenge in today's society. Some of the drivers clearly fall within the box marked 'benefits'; that is, there is a clearly identified and unequivocal advantage, both to organizations and individuals, to be gained from better understanding the nature of diversity. However, as will be seen later in this chapter, for many organizations and individuals diversity is a particularly difficult concept to grasp, and for some it is seen as a direct challenge to long-held individual views and attitudes.

In this chapter we also describe the legal framework and how this is progressing diversity within our society, and identify the particular business benefits that will be enjoyed by those organizations that effectively manage diversity (and the potential for increased benefits that would result if diversity were embraced and eventually celebrated).

Before moving on to these discussions, let us take some time to consider where you stand on the issues.

What do you understand by the term 'diversity'?

Why should individuals and organizations be concerned with managing diversity (whether from an organizational or an individual perspective)?

WHAT DIVERSITY MEANS

In almost all of the training we have done with organizations, participants have been challenged to say what diversity means to them. One group we worked with came up with the idea that diversity is the 'avoidance of mono-culture'. Such a straightforward definition has many positive characteristics. It speaks of actively working against a situation where everyone is assumed to be the same and with similar needs. In a mono-cultural situation assumptions are often made on the basis of the values, attitudes, beliefs and behaviour of the majority group. Training in diversity is essentially working towards challenging those assumptions and finding ways of avoiding their often-negative outcomes.

It is probably of little surprise that there are a number of views as to what constitutes diversity. Definitions range from functional descriptions to humanistic statements advocating acceptance of 'otherness' and to fairly detailed and inclusive analyses that embrace personal qualities and characteristics.

For example, the California Department of Education acknowledges the challenge of diversity and notes, 'we are distinguished and united by differences and similarities according to gender, age, language, culture, race, sexual identity and income level' (www.cde.ca.gov/iasa/diversity.html).

A broader definition is offered by the University of Maryland:

> Diversity is 'otherness', or those human qualities that are different from our own and outside the groups to which we belong, yet are present in other individuals and groups.

> (University of Maryland, 1995, www.inform.umd.edu)

This particular definition is further extended to add what are described as primary and secondary dimensions. In this regard primary dimensions include features such as age, ethnicity, gender, physical abilities, race and sexual orientation. Secondary dimensions are features which are capable of change and might include education, place of residence, class, marital status, religious beliefs, occupational status and life experiences.

The United Nations (UN) offers a comprehensive definition which in many ways highlights the complexity of this area:

> Diversity takes many forms. It is usually thought of in terms of obvious attributes – age differences, race, gender, physical ability, sexual orientation, religion and language. Diversity in terms of background professional experience, skills and specialization, values and culture, as well as social class, is a prevailing pattern.
>
> (United Nations, 2000)

The UN paper also acknowledges the link between diversity and other external factors such as globalization and technological advances, and notes that the management of diversity should also take account of more individual and personal characteristics such as family position, personality and job function: 'in short, all characteristics that go into the shaping of individual perspectives'. However, the UN notes that for some the term 'diversity' is seen as a new buzzword for equal opportunities, while others see it as the antithesis of equal opportunities. It argues that:

> Diversity management should thus be viewed as an inclusive concept, encompassing a broader focus than employment equity would suggest. It requires one to look at the mindset and the culture of an organization and the different perspectives people bring to an organization on account of their ethnicity, social background, professional values, styles, disabilities or other differences.
>
> (United Nations, 2000)

We have found the richness of this particular definition to be particularly useful when dealing with far-ranging cultural change programmes. However, this is often an area where we have been challenged, and in cases where our ethical and moral argument for more effective diversity management has failed to convince sceptics, we have found that a number of external factors can be a successful means of persuading cynics that effective diversity management is an essential component of any successful organization.

Challenges	Benefits

Figure 2.1 *Challenges and benefits*

Before looking at some of these factors, take a little time to identify some of the challenges and benefits that could be associated with diversity management.

You may have included the following:

Challenges	Benefits
Convincing all stakeholders that diversity is inevitable	Greater workforce unity and productivity
Marketing the benefits of diversity management (costs are easier to quantify than benefits)	Widening the suite of performance indicators to include qualitative measures as well as purely financial (for example the balanced scorecard)
Existing employees may feel threatened or resentful and may perceive that recruitment and promotion opportunities have been reduced	Employment conditions can be developed to meet individual needs and aspirations (as opposed to one size fits all)

Figure 2.2 *Examples of challenges and benefits*

Whatever the drivers for diversity, the UN identified five qualities which contribute to the successful management of diversity:

- **Leadership:** demonstrable commitment and support including the establishment of steering and advisory groups and effective communication plans.
- **Valid and reliable performance measurements:** pan-organizational assessments, benchmarking and comparative analyses.
- **Education:** awareness training complemented by advanced training, development of in-house expertise.
- **Cultural and management change:** devising and implementing effective human resource management strategies.
- **Follow up:** longitudinal evaluation, performance management systems and knowledge management.

What is clear from the above is that effective management of diversity cannot be achieved by training alone; it needs a comprehensive and systematic approach, one which is subject to constant evaluation and assessment and takes account of a range of extraneous issues. We will now look in more detail at some of the external factors for more effective diversity management.

THE BUSINESS CASE FOR DIVERSITY

There is little doubt that the vast majority of private sector companies are concerned with profitability and increasing the bottom line. This can be achieved in a number of ways including:

- reducing operational costs while maintaining levels of output and profitability (less input for same output);
- increasing productivity and profitability while maintaining existing levels of input (more output for same input);
- reducing non-operational costs and overheads while maintaining levels of input and output (doing things smarter);
- reducing non-operational costs and overheads while maintaining levels of input and increasing levels of output (doing things even smarter).

You can probably think of some more sophisticated examples, but what is clear is that while there is a commercial driver for companies to become even more profitable, there is a similar need for public sector and not-for-profit organizations to become more effective and efficient. Government is increasingly concerned to make more effective use of public money, and there is a far greater emphasis within the public sector on such issues as accountability, value for money, performance management and increased efficiency.

In this section we look in more detail at the business drivers for diversity, and in particular we try to identify examples of how a better understanding of diversity can make organizations do things smarter and in some cases even smarter (to make private sector companies more profitable and public sector organizations more efficient and effective).

Our people are our most important resource

How often have we seen these or similar words printed in glossy annual reports or strategic plans? Are the words the product of clever wordsmithing and merely presentational, or do they actually represent the strategic intentions of an organization which will result in clear specific actions and outcomes?

The most forward-looking organizations are those that have recognized the changing demographics of their workforces and are actively seeking to develop their organizational competences so that they recruit, retain and develop the highest-calibre staff. The key competence in this regard, both from an organizational perspective and for individuals, is the ability to manage effectively a diverse workforce. Have a look at the following scenarios and think about the issues they generate.

- Ron is 61 years old. He has taken early retirement having worked for 40 years in the engineering industry. He would like to remain active in his retirement and would like some form of non-manual part-time work. He has unsuccessfully applied for several jobs as a part-time filing clerk, and when he asked why he had not been interviewed he was told that he was too old.
- Michelle is a 25-year-old black woman who would like to join the Prison Service. However, having read a series of newspaper reports detailing allegations of racial harassment against prisoners, she is not sure whether this is the career for her.
- Paul is a 22-year-old gay man working in a small manufacturing company. At his last annual appraisal his line manager asked him about his personal circumstances and whether or not he was ready to settle down and start a family.

- Sue is a 35-year-old woman working in the financial industry. For the past three years she has been one of the top-earning traders in her department, having achieved year-on-year profit growth 35 per cent above the average. In the last two years less-profitable traders have been promoted above her, and almost all traders in her department have received significantly greater end of year bonuses.

What is the significance of the above scenarios and how do they relate to the bottom line? Consider the following:

- In 2003–04 over 115,000 applications for Employment Tribunal were received.
- In the same year, sex discrimination cases rose by 75 per cent.
- The average award for race discrimination cases is £26,660.
- In 2003–04 3.8 million parents in the UK are eligible to exercise flexible working rights.
- In 2011 it is projected that 25 per cent of women and 21 per cent of men will be aged 60 or over.
- In 2011 it is projected that women will comprise 46 per cent of the labour force.
- A recent survey of private sector employment equality practices in Scotland found the following:
  - Around 60 per cent of respondents initiated equal opportunity programmes because their competitors had already implemented equality programmes.
  - Over 80 per cent of respondents initiated programmes because of the prospect of being involved in an industrial tribunal.
  - Approximately 90 per cent of respondents felt that it was quite or very important to be seen to be forward looking.
  - Almost 60 per cent expressed the desire to be demonstrating good practice.
- In the United States it was forecast that between 1985 and 2000, 85 per cent of entrants to the workforce would be 'women, minorities and immigrants'.
- African-Americans currently comprise 10.1 per cent of the United States' 112.4 million employed civilians. However, the same group comprise 6.2 per cent of managers and 8.5 per cent of technical and support staff.

DIVERSITY AND THE BOTTOM LINE

At the beginning of this section we indicated that a successful diversity management programme could improve profitability, but exactly how can this be achieved? Consider Table 2.1.

What also needs to be taken into account is the cost of the 'do nothing' option. Specific examples might be the costs of litigation for failing to comply with the legislation or the potential loss of revenue from a damaged corporate image.

While it is important that organizations develop effective policies and procedures (and in this regard the Commission for Racial Equality has developed a useful template: see www.cre.gov.uk), it is absolutely essential that these strategies be turned into tangible and measurable actions. We will be looking in more detail at diversity strategies later in this chapter. However, it is important to note that the smarter organizations will have developed most or all of the following in relation to *all* potential employees:

- recruitment targets at all levels of the organization;
- awareness training for *all* staff;
- non-discriminatory recruitment, promotion and reward systems;
- flexible working arrangements;
- constant and effective monitoring and evaluation of their management of diversity.

If we have failed to convince you that there is a business case for managing diversity (we sincerely hope that you believe it is the right thing to do in any case!), then you might also wish to examine the existing legal framework.

THE ETHICAL CASE FOR DIVERSITY

As we have discussed above, there is an increasingly sound business case being made for responding effectively to diversity. In this section we look at the issue from an ethical perspective. In other words, even if there were no effective business case for responding to diversity we would still be left with the reality that there is an ethical imperative for doing so. This case also stands outside the legal framework that will be discussed later. In short, responding to the diversity of our society is based simply in the fact that it is the right thing to do. As the philosopher Iris Murdoch once put it, ethics is essentiality about the 'sovereignty of the good'. We respond to diversity not

Table 2.1   *Organizational dimensions of diversity*

Perception/issue	Corporate responsibility	Being smarter
The organization is seen by job seekers as institutionally racist or sexist	Branding and imaging	In times of prosperity and low employment job seekers can afford to be selective. The more successful organizations will be those that can position themselves as 'employers of choice' and increase their ability to recruit the highest potential applicants.
The organization's initial selection process is seen by applicants to be discriminatory	Recruitment policies and processes	Assessment processes must be capable of identifying and selecting the best candidate for the position regardless of colour, nationality, gender, sexual orientation or age.
The organizational culture is seen as one which accepts and encourages discriminatory practice and behaviour	Organizational policies and management practice	Employees will achieve greater productivity if they work in a non-discriminatory and harassment free work-place. More flexible policies and working practices will increase the potential skills pool from which organizations are trying to recruit.

Table 2.1   *(Continued)*

Perception/issue	Corporate responsibility	Being smarter
		Managers' time is more productive if directed towards managing performance rather than addressing discriminatory behaviour.
The organizational promotion structure and system are seen as unfair	Organizational policies and promotion, pay and reward systems	As with recruitment processes, the system for promotion and rewards must be non-discriminatory and focused on promoting and rewarding the best employees. Recruitment is an expensive overhead: the smarter organizations are those that can retain the best-performing staff.

simply because it will make organizations work better, or even because the law or human rights conventions say we must; we respond because it is the right thing to do.

Mature adults will, by default, work within ethical frameworks, although they may be very different. We all have a sense of what is right and what is wrong, but very often the decisions that we make in relation to diversity issues are made in the context of different ethical frameworks.

------------------------- **Pause for reflection** -------------------------

What is your position on issues such as:

- abortion;
- euthanasia ;
- capital punishment;
- immigration;
- asylum;
- homosexuality;
- the role of women in society.

What framework of decision making do you use?

Ethics has to do with the frameworks we use to come to make judgements. A study of ethics helps us to decide and determine the principles by which such decisions are made.

Beabout and Wennemann (1994: 13) outline a number of prominent theories of ethics. In summary these are:

- Egoism – the view that the best course of action to be taken in a given situation is governed by self-interest.
- Conventional morality – the view that the standard for determining right and wrong is to be governed by the conventional rules and practices of society. In many ways this is as problematic as a framework for responding to diversity because of the assumptions that may be attached to the culture of the majority group in a particular society.
- Utilitarianism – the ethical approach that says that a particular course of action or decision should be the one that generates the greatest good for the greatest number of people.
- Duty ethics – the view that duty is the highest and ultimate standard. An action is morally right if it is done solely for the sake of duty.
- Virtue – the ethics of virtue have their roots in the work of the Greek philosophers Plato and Aristotle. Aristotle saw virtue as a state of character which developed as a result of wisdom, justice, temperance and prudence.

Each of these approaches to ethics is problematic in one way or another and does not fully capture the ethical imperatives surrounding responses to diversity. For example, a utilitarian approach to diversity might lead to treating all people in exactly the same way. To treat people equally however, may, of necessity, mean treating them according to their needs. So to do something, or to make a decision, according to a utilitarian ethical framework may have the exact opposite effect to that intended in that a majority group could be advantaged (ie the good of the greatest number of people) over a minority (a smaller number of people).

Drawing on the ideas of Neyroud and Beckley (2001: 47–8) we might consider eight principles for ethical professional behaviour and decision making. As you study them, consider how they may relate to your own professional context and whether they adequately capture how and why a given individual might respond to others with fairness and non-discrimination.

1. *Respect for personal autonomy*. In other words, a respect for the fact that people have a right to be who they are. This would include respecting their rights as citizen and treating each person with dignity and respect.
2. *Beneficence*. Active goodness or kindness.
3. *Non-malfeasance*. In other words, not being involved in wrongdoing. Such an ethical approach in terms of diversity would mean the practice of proactive antidiscrimination and standing up for what you believe.
4. *Justice*. Delivering your professional service, whether as a trainer, manager or other service delivery, according to need, with a high value on human rights and legality.
5. *Responsibility*. People have personal responsibility for their actions and need to be able to justify *why* they do what they do.
6. *Care*. There is a natural human response of care towards each other.
7. *Honesty*. Not simply confined to honesty in dealing with others, but also in the veracity of one's own self-reflection in relation to the issues.
8. *Stewardship*. There must be a careful and attentive focus on the stewardship of powers over others in society. This would include the power that trainers have, the power that managers have in organizations, as well as direct power that people may have over others in society.

Pause for reflection

Consider the ethical principles outlined above. How do they fit with your own approach to diversity issues?

As we have noted elsewhere in the book, people who purport to train others in relation to diversity both need to, and need to be seen to, 'walk the talk'.

This will inevitably involve thinking through your personal ethical framework and being confident of your own ethical case.

THE LEGAL FRAMEWORK FOR DIVERSITY

In this section we will briefly examine the most recent legislation concerned with diversity issues. We recommend that you examine in greater detail the legislation, any supporting codes of practice, and the emerging guidelines and briefing papers. The relevant legislation in this regard includes:

- The Employment Equality (Sexual Orientation) Regulations 2003
- The Employment Equality (Religion or Belief) Regulations 2003
- Race Relations (Amendment) Act 2000;
- Human Rights Act 1998;
- Article 13 of the Treaty of Amsterdam;
- Sex Discrimination Act 1975;
- Disability Discrimination Act 1995.

The Employment Equality (Sexual Orientation) Regulations 2003 and the Employment Equality (Religion or Belief) Regulations 2003 outlaw discrimination in employment and vocational training on the grounds of sexual orientation and religion or belief respectively. The Regulations also implement strands of the European Employment Directive (Council Directive 2000/78/EC).

Similar to the Race Relations Act 1976, these Regulations make it unlawful to discriminate against someone in the workplace on the grounds of:

- direct discrimination – treating people less favourably than others on grounds of sexual orientation or religion or belief;
- indirect discrimination – applying a provision, criterion or practice which disadvantages people of a particular sexual orientation or religion or belief and which is not justified as a proportionate means of achieving a legitimate aim;
- harassment – unwanted conduct that violates people's dignity or creates an intimidating, hostile, degrading, humiliating or offensive environment;
- victimization – treating people less favourably because of something they have done under or in connection with the Regulations, eg made a formal complaint of discrimination or given evidence in a tribunal case.

The Sexual Orientation Regulations apply to discrimination, both actual and perceived, on the grounds of orientation towards persons of the same sex (lesbians and gays), the opposite sex (heterosexuals) and the same and opposite sex (bisexuals).

The Religion or Belief Regulations apply to discrimination, both actual and perceived, on grounds of religion, religious belief or similar philosophical belief.

Both Regulations also cover association, ie being discriminated against on grounds of the sexual orientation or religion or belief of those with whom the person associates such as friends and/or family (for more information: www.dti.gov.uk).

Race Relations (Amendment) Act 2000

This Act amends the Race Relations Act 1976 and makes it unlawful to discriminate against anyone on grounds of race, colour, nationality (including citizenship), or ethnic or national origin. The amended Act also imposes on a number of public authorities a general duty to promote racial equality in the following areas:

- jobs;
- training;
- housing;
- education;
- the provision of goods, facilities and services.

Additionally the amended Act makes it unlawful for public bodies (such as government departments) to discriminate while executing any of their functions, and places on a number of public bodies a general duty to promote equality of opportunity and good race relations.

General duties

The 2000 Act places on a number of listed public authorities, including the Scottish Administration, the Welsh Assembly, the National Health Service, local authorities, police authorities and the armed services, the general duty described above. It is anticipated that a further 300 public authorities will be added to this list by the Home Secretary.

In complying with the general duty the listed authorities need to ensure that existing policies and practices do not disadvantage any ethnic minority groups, and in formulating any new policies they need to consider racial equality implications, in most cases using a consultation process.

Some of the listed authorities are required to undertake certain specified duties to assist with the application of the general duty. Specified duties include ethnic monitoring of the workforce, consultation regarding proposed policies, and monitoring the impact of current policies and procedures on race equality.

As a result of the new Act, the Commission for Racial Equality (CRE) has provided a Code of Practice to provide guidance on complying with the general and specific duties. The CRE also has powers to enforce the specific duties, and in cases of non-compliance to apply to a county court (or sheriff court in Scotland) for a legally binding compliance order.

The Human Rights Act 1998

The Human Rights Act (HRA) 1998 is a means for incorporating the European Convention on Human Rights (ECHR) into the UK legal framework. Of particular relevance here are Sections 1 and 6 of the HRA. Section 1HRA specifies the ECHR Articles and Protocols which have been adopted by the UK government. Section 6 makes it unlawful for a public authority to act in a way that is incompatible with European Convention Rights.

Of particular note is ECHR Article 14 which prohibits discrimination on the grounds of sex, colour, language, religion, national or social origin, association with a national minority, property, birth or political or other opinion. However an infringement against any of the grounds mentioned in Article 14 cannot be claimed in its own right and must be claimed in conjunction with infringements against other Articles. While the Article fails to provide an overarching criminalization of discrimination, more extreme cases of racial or sexual harassment might amount to an infringement of Article 3 (inhuman or degrading treatment).

Article 13 of the Treaty of Amsterdam

In 2000 the Council of Ministers of the European Union (EU) adopted three new measures, based on Article 13 of the Treaty of Amsterdam, to tackle discrimination within the member states. Although the principles of Article 13 are not legally binding, the EU proposes to adopt two additional directives covering minimum standards of legal protection against discrimination and an anti-discrimination Action Plan. Article 13 comprises an Employment Directive and a Race Directive. The Employment Directive requires EU member states to make discrimination unlawful in the areas of training and employment on the grounds of religion or belief, disability, age or sexual orientation.

The Race Directive (note similarities with the Race Relations (Amendment) Act 2000) requires member states to make discrimination on the grounds of racial or ethnic origin unlawful in the areas of employment, training, education, access to social security and health care, social advantages and access to goods and services, including housing.[1]

The Action Plan aims to promote cooperation between the member states in tackling discrimination, and runs for six years from 2001.

Sex Discrimination Act 1975

The Sex Discrimination Act (SDA) 1975 was amended and widened in 1986; it should be read in conjunction with the Equal Pay Act (EPA) 1984. The SDA makes it unlawful to discriminate against people on the grounds of their gender. The SDA applies to two kinds of discrimination: direct discrimination (that is, treating someone unfairly because of their gender) and indirect discrimination (that is, applying conditions which at face value appear to apply to everyone, but in fact discriminate against some people because of their gender) in a number of areas, including:

- employment;
- education;
- advertising;
- the provision of housing, goods or services.

Additionally it is unlawful to discriminate against people because of their marital status in respect of employment conditions or in job advertisements. However in specific cases certain jobs may have Genuine Occupational Qualifications (GOQs) where it is lawful to specify that the job must be undertaken by a member of a certain sex (for example, female toilet attendant).

The EPA applies to pay and other contractual factors where both men and women are undertaking similar work, work which is deemed to be equivalent (for example in terms of grading) or work which has equal value.

Disability Discrimination Act 1995

The Disability Discrimination Act provides a number of laws and measures with the intention of ending discriminatory acts against disabled people in a number of areas, including:

- employment;
- the provision of services and goods;
- buying or renting land or property.

Additionally the Act requires educational establishments to provide information for disabled people, and allows the government to set minimum standards in respect of public transport and to set up the National Disability Council and the Northern Ireland Disability Council.

The law makes it illegal for employers to treat a disabled person less favourably than someone else because of his or her disability, and applies to all aspects of employment, including recruitment, training, promotion and dismissal.[2] The Act also applies to any organization or individual who provides goods, facilities or services, on payment or otherwise, to the public (for example, shops, municipal swimming pools or libraries). It is against the law[3] for service providers to:

- refuse to serve someone because of his or her disability;
- offer a lower standard of service or goods to a disabled person than that offered to others;
- provide a service to a disabled person which is different from the terms offered to other people;
- provide services in a way in which it is impossible or unreasonably difficult for a disabled person to use the service or goods.

The Act also makes it illegal for anyone selling land or property to unreasonably discriminate against a person because of his or her disability.

In addition to using new legislation as a lever for change, government can call upon public inquiries and other pan-government reform programmes as part of its change programme. Two such reform initiatives are the Stephen Lawrence Inquiry and the government modernization programme.

The Stephen Lawrence Inquiry

There is little doubt that the Stephen Lawrence Inquiry was a landmark in the development of criminal justice in the United Kingdom. However, its impact is even more far-reaching, as noted by the Home Secretary in his Action Plan: 'progress on policing must be part of a wider context. We have a commitment to building an anti-racist society.' The Inquiry, following the racist murder of a South London youth, was led by Sir William Macpherson and the final report was particularly damning of the police service in a number of areas. Macpherson's report not only served to expose police failures, it also accused the organization of being institutionally racist, which was defined as:

> The collective failure of an organization to provide an appropriate and professional service to people because of their colour, culture or ethnic origin. It can be seen or detected in processes, attitudes and behaviour which amount to unwitting prejudice, ignorance, thoughtlessness and racist stereotyping which disadvantage minority ethnic people.

> (Macpherson, 1999: para 6.34)

Macpherson came to his conclusion after considering four fundamental factors:

• The murder investigations, including police treatment of Stephen's family and witnesses to his murder, and the failure of many investigating officers to recognize that his murder was racially motivated.
• The disparity between the numbers of ethnic minority people and majority white people stopped and searched by the police.
• National 'under-reporting' of racial incidents, which Macpherson concluded was due to an inadequate police response and an absence of confidence in victims to report such incidents.
• Failures in police training, particularly in respect of community and race awareness.

As noted above, such failures are not the exclusive domain of the police service, and subsequently a number of other public sector organizations have been described as being institutionally racist. But how does your own organization fare? Taking into account the four factors noted above, try answering the questions in Figure 2.3.

The reforms instigated by the Home Office to the criminal justice system are also part of a wide-ranging modernization programme instigated by the government, and we will now examine the impact of this agenda on diversity.

THE GOVERNMENT MODERNIZATION AGENDA

In its far-reaching proposals to modernize government, the 1999 White Paper *Modernizing Government* sets out its stall:

Question	Response
1. Does your organization deliver lower levels of service to ethnic minority customers or clients?	
2. Does your organization use inappropriate stereotyping of ethnic minority groups?	
3. Does your organization enjoy the absolute confidence of ethnic minority groups?	
4. Does your organization have in place a comprehensive diversity awareness training programme?	

Figure 2.3 *Modernizing government checklist*

We must accelerate progress on diversity if this country is to get the public services it needs for the new millennium. The public service must be a part of, not apart from the society it serves.

(HM Government Cabinet Office, 1999)

A subsequent paper on reforming the civil service developed this theme further:

We need a civil service that is genuinely diverse. Only a truly diverse service will be capable of delivering the policies and services which our diverse society is entitled to expect. To be really effective the service must make the fullest use of its people, give them the chance to play their part, develop and progress to the maximum of their potential.

(HM Government Cabinet Office, 1999)

A strategic plan to tackle these issues proposed a number of mandatory actions in the following areas:

* awareness;
* leadership;

- management capability;
- equal opportunities.

As part of this plan, individual departments are required as part of their own planning processes to build the mandatory actions into internal action plans and to provide regular reports on progress.

Such far-reaching government policies result from a recognition that effective management of diversity can provide access to a much wider pool of talent, and that an even wider phenomenon is allowing that pool of talent to become more mobile and able to work within a wider international scale. That phenomenon is globalization.

GLOBALIZATION AND THE RECRUITMENT AND RETENTION OF STAFF

Globalization is a relatively new term to describe a trend which has played a significant part in world history. Today globalization is often associated with the worldwide marketing of huge corporations and their symbols such as the McDonald's logo (more than 25,000 outlets in approximately 120 countries), or with the large-scale demonstrations and outbreaks of violent disorder at International Monetary Fund meetings and anti-capitalist protests. However, it could be argued that the Roman Empire and similar empires built by Spain, Portugal, Britain and Holland were attempts to devise a global trading market as well as extend the nation state. These quite extensive empires have since collapsed, and subsequently as a result of the two world wars in the last century and the 1930s depression, many nation states refocused energy into home-based markets rather than looking towards international trade. A prevailing issue at this point in time was a growing realization that international trading could result in a number of disbenefits, including home-based unemployment and increased poverty.

More recent events, including the development of democracies in the former Eastern Bloc Communist countries, and technological developments such as the internet and telecommunications, have led to the removal of protectionist barriers and the expansion of companies into new countries – the process of globalization. Critics of globalization see it as a deliberate attempt to control the world's political economy, involving the internationalization of finance, government and countries' populations. But what are the implications for managing diversity?

As part of its own future planning, the UK government has identified globalization as one of the six key drivers of change which will impact on government over the next decades. This view takes the following points into account.

It is almost certain that the world's population will rapidly expand over the next decades. With the world's population increasing annually by some 90 million, it is predicted that by 2050 the population could stand at 8.9 billion as compared to the 6 billion today. All of the anticipated growth is expected to occur in the developing world. By 2020 the developed world will house one-fifth of the world's total population, as compared with one-third in 1950 and one quarter today. Such demographic changes will also lead to increased trading, although trading is also expected to increase in its own right.

It is accepted by all of the main international economic institutions that the developing countries will see an increase in their share of world output, and that capital markets and capital flows will increase as the costs of transactions are reduced. As organizations become more global and trading is further liberalized, with an increasing number of developing-world countries becoming part of the globalization phenomenon, the need for more effective diversity management becomes increasingly apparent. In this regard the issues can be separated into two areas: those concerning UK nationals and those concerning non-UK nationals.

UK nationals

The United Kingdom has witnessed a significant shift in emphasis to its industrial landscape over the past two decades. Previous reliance on mining, the steel industry and to a lesser extent manufacturing has been replaced by growth in telecommunications, support services and retail sectors. As UK organizations become more global, workers will increasingly be expected to work with and in other countries. As organizations develop a 'one company, one team' philosophy, the organizational culture is likely to be one which is company driven rather than one which reflects the national culture of the parent company.

HSBC, the world's second largest bank, has recently embarked on an ambitious strategic plan 'Managing for Growth', which places effective diversity management at its core. An extensive marketing campaign re-assured customers and potential customers of the ability of HSBC to understand the needs of its customers and their communities. The need to identify with and relate to divergent cultures and communities is highlighted by the following:

> The old ways of looking at the global economy are no longer relevant. The world has dynamic areas including the USA and Asia excluding Japan, and stagnant areas, primarily Japan and the eurozone. We assess the new world order, highlighting six key misunderstandings. Our conclusions? China is already a consumer powerhouse. Commodity prices are high because labour costs are low. Companies have escaped the economic clutches of their host countries. Japan and Germany should be regarded as capital providers, not repressed consumers. Oil prices are permanently higher but inflation need not be. And monetary policies across regions will increasingly diverge. (www.hsbc.com)

While globalization and diversity present some issues for UK nationals, for non-UK nationals the issues are slightly different.

Non-UK nationals

At the time of writing, and following the lead-in to a general election in the UK, the issue of immigration and asylum is the subject of heated debate. On the one hand there is an acknowledgement that the UK is facing a serious skills shortage both in professions such as health and education and in market sectors such as construction and services. As noted by the *Guardian* (*source:* www.guardian.co.uk/immigration), recent research found that 10 per cent of construction employers had employed workers from the most recently joined European Union member states. Additionally 8 per cent of new workers in the hotel and retail sectors came from a similar background, whilst 7 per cent of companies in the finance and business services sector had recruited at least one employee from a country that had recently joined the EU. At a time when some political parties have attempted to blur the distinction between immigration and asylum-seeking it is interesting to note that since Poland joined the EU in May 2004, just over 73,500 Polish nationals have signed the British government register of migrant workers: while almost half of that figure comprise new immigrants, the remainder were illegal workers who have registered in order to legitimize their continued presence in Britain. However, it is not just the UK that is examining its immigration policies.

Across Europe a number of countries are in the process of examining their approaches to immigration and, alongside systems designed to reduce illegal immigration, sit policies designed to encourage and regulate immigration of skilled workers. It also appears to be the case that public opinion supports a tougher stance on immigration. A survey published in March 2005 signified that over 60 per cent of respondents supported a five-year plan developed by the European Union designed to improve cooperation on immigration and asylum policy. This stance is also reflected in internal policies, with the French Interior Minister announcing tough measures to reduce the number of illegal immigrants estimated to range between 200,000 and 400,000. Also Germany, which has a population of approximately 7.3 million foreigners, at least 500,000 of whom are illegal, introduced legislation intended to encourage the legal entry of highly skilled workers and to deport those without valid papers. However, it is Austria that has perhaps taken the toughest stance: considered by many to have the most restrictive asylum laws in Europe, recent legalization now means that that asylum seekers on hunger strike will be force fed (*source:* www.eubusiness.com).

The balance in this regard is to encourage the immigration of skilled workers in order to meet the skills shortage, and to reduce opportunities for illegal migrants. In this regard it seems likely that the UK will adopt a points system similar to those developed in Canada and Australia where applicants are judged on their ability to contribute to the national economy. The Centre for Economic Performance (CEP) at the London School of Economics argue that immigration does not threaten the jobs or salary rates of UK residents, rather it results in a number of financial benefits, for example by providing extra funds for pension schemes. Their study also found that whilst immigration rates were increasing, this was the result of a strong economy rather than a weak immigration policy (*source:* http://news.scotsman.com/politics. cfm?id=423312005).

The extent of the skills shortage has been emphasized in a number of areas. For example, the CEP report discussed above suggests that the shortfall of teachers, currently 34,000 in England and Wales, may become critical as a result of early retirement and resignation to pursue other careers. The nursing profession is experiencing similar challenges, with the Royal College of Nursing predicting that 24 per cent of registered nurses will be retiring within five years. Faced with a current shortfall of just over 9,000, an overseas recruitment drive proved to be particularly successful and in 2004 40 per cent of new entrants to the profession came from outside of the UK. Moreover it has been estimated that 10,000 new GPs will be needed to implement the government's health plan. With only 110 having been recruited in the previous year it is perhaps of greater concern that 20–30 per cent of GPs intend to retire before the age of 60 and many consultants are retiring around the age of 60 instead of 65 (*source:* www.advisorybodies.doh.gov.uk).

However, it also appears that global marketization is helping to address the skills shortage and it is interesting to note the approach of Atkins, one of the UK's largest suppliers of government services: faced with an acute shortage of skilled workers that jeopardized its work on developing the West Coast mainline for Network Rail, Atkins have employed 500 Chinese workers to help deliver this £7.5 billion project. The staff worked from offices in Shenzhen and Beijing, developing signalling systems which were then delivered electronically to Britain.

Clearly there are a number of external features, different areas of legislation and human factors which together make up a more complete picture of diversity. However, where do previous initiatives, such as equal opportunities or race awareness, now stand and is it the case that the various pieces of legislation in the UK are in competition with one another?

DIVERSITY/RACE EQUALITY/EQUAL OPPORTUNITIES/ COMMUNITY AND RACE RELATIONS/FAIRNESS: WHERE THE FOCUS SHOULD BE

Our work in this area began in the mid-1980s, when the focus was very much on community and race relations training. Since then our work has been rebranded as equal opportunities, fairness for all and now diversity. But are there any fundamental differences? In this next exercise, outline what you understand by the terms in Figure 2.4.

We have found the equality opportunities and diversity continuum in Table 2.2 (adapted from one devised by the Civil Service) a useful way of categorizing the various terms as well as providing a developmental framework for organizational and individual learning.

For us diversity embraces all of the elements of community and race relations, equal opportunities, race awareness, fair treatment and more. However, one difficulty with this inclusive approach is the potential for one component of diversity to be marginalized in favour of another. Furthermore, some single-interest groups can demand that their particular issue is seen as more important than others. This is not always an easy area to address. However, we have found that a systematic approach to policy and strategy implementation is most likely to be successful, and we now look

Term	Description
Community and race relations	
Race equality	
Fair treatment	
Diversity	

Figure 2.4 *Diversity terms*

Table 2.2 *Equal opportunities and diversity continuum*

Main focus	Descriptor
Basic equal opportunities	Training will focus on race, gender, disability and religious beliefs and on the legal requirements.
Further development of equal opportunities	The intention here is to develop understanding rather than impart knowledge. Exercises will encourage participants to view and experience activities as a minority and to plan how they can help change cultural barriers to minority advancement. At an organizational level perception/ attitude surveys would attempt to measure levels of perceived fairness.
Emerging diversity	Here the focus is on difference. As well as race, gender and disability, other factors which could be disadvantageous are introduced such as accent, educational background, sexual orientation and age. Training is aimed at increasing levels of awareness, acknowledging majority fears and identifying ways of confronting them.

Table 2.2   *(Continued)*

Main focus	Descriptor
Basic diversity	At this level the focus is on valuing individuals and their differences and translating this attitude into workplace behaviours.
	At an organizational level perception/ attitude surveys would be used to measure the extent to which diversity is valued.
Mainstreaming diversity	New values are constantly reaffirmed, the organization is supported to achieve long-term cultural change.
	Planning processes and performance measurement systems continually monitor performance. Long-term evaluation studies are complemented by benchmarking.

briefly at ways of implementing organizational change programmes.

ORGANIZATIONAL STRATEGIES

In the previous sections we have described a variety of drivers that have caused a number of organizations to rethink their approach to managing diversity. The combined effects of the new legislation, the Macpherson Inquiry and the business benefits have led to a number of organizations, both public and private sector, revisiting their strategic and business planning processes. But exactly how do you ensure that managing diversity becomes a central part of the organizational structure and its processes?

One method is that advocated by the Commission for Racial Equality (CRE). Its 10-point plan involves:

- developing policies to cover recruitment, training and promotion;
- action plans with specific and measurable targets;

- pan-organizational awareness training, and additional training for those staff involved in recruitment, selection and training;
- an organizational diversity audit to establish the current position and enable progress to be monitored;
- a review of all recruitment, selection, promotion and training processes;
- the production of job descriptions for all roles;
- where appropriate the offer of pre-employment training to prepare job applicants for selection tests and interviews, and consideration of positive action to encourage under-represented groups to apply for vacancies;
- consideration of the organizational image and determination of whether or not a more positive image could be presented;
- consideration of more flexible working arrangements and determination of what specialist equipment is required for disabled employees;
- the development of closer links with local community groups, schools and other organizations.

However, while this provides a comprehensive framework, it is acknowledged by the CRE that policies alone will not bring about effective diversity management. It has been said that 80 per cent of strategic plans are unsuccessful, so what can be done to ensure that diversity strategies or policies are successfully implemented? One method that is reaping rewards in both the public and private sectors is an approach developed by the Office for Government Commerce (OGC) (formerly the Central Computer and Telecommunications Agency).

Managing Successful Programmes

Managing Successful Programmes (MSP) was developed as a complementary process to one previously developed to manage and implement projects successfully (known as PRINCE2 (Projects in a Controlled Environment)). MSP comprises a number of processes to ensure that large-scale programmes of change, such as a diversity strategy, are effectively implemented, by providing a systematic approach to managing the portfolio of projects which will deliver the intended benefits. MSP is built around a number of processes as shown in Figure 2.5.

Consider the model in Figure 2.6, which we developed for a large public sector organization. This framework enabled us to take a strategic view of the direction and progress of the programme while at the same time being reassured that the project controls would ensure that the project outcomes would be delivered on time and fit for purpose. While project and

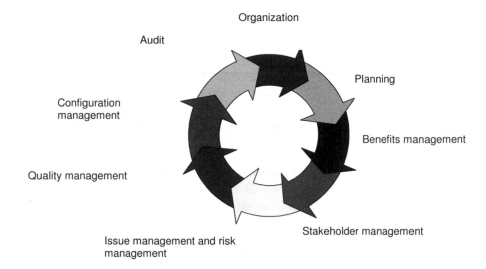

Organization

Audit

Planning

Configuration
management

Benefits management

Quality management

Stakeholder management

Issue management and risk
management

- *Programmed management organization*
  giving people clear roles, responsibilities, leadership and lines of communication. There is a *Sponsoring Group* of senior executives including the *Programme Director* with ultimate accountability

- *Programme planning*
  using a *Programme Plan* to ensure that control is established and maintained

- *Benefits management*
  identifying, optimizing and tracking expected benefits to ensure they are achieved

- *Stakeholder management*
  ensuring all interested parties are appropriately involved in the programme

- *Issue management and risk management*
  having a strategy for dealing with current and anticipated problems

- *Quality management*
  ensuring that the end products of the programme are fit for purpose

- *Configuration management*
  keeping monitoring information about the programme up to date and accurate

- *Audit*
  ensuring that technical, statutory, contract and accounting standards are used

Source: OGC, 1999

Figure 2.5   *The principles of programme management*

programme management is sometimes seen as an unnecessary overhead, there are a number of organizations that see successful project and programme management as the key to successful organizations.

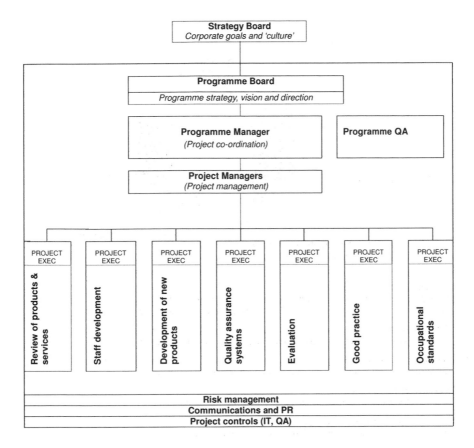

Figure 2.6 *An MSP model for a large organization*

CONCLUSION

In this chapter we have outlined a number of factors that are driving the need for more effective diversity of management. It is our belief that recognition of diversity is a fundamental moral human right. However, we acknowledge that for some it is seen as a challenge, and we briefly set out a business case for diversity. We then described the current legal framework and the impact of globalization.

Once an organization has committed to diversity there is a need to identify how organizational change will be achieved, and in the next chapter we will examine in more detail how to learn about diversity.

KEY LEARNING POINTS

In this chapter we asked you to consider a number of issues which are driving forward the requirement for a greater emphasis on diversity training.

- We noted that a number of different definitions of diversity are available, ranging from the humanistic 'oneness' approach to functional and detailed definitions which take account of class, education and wealth as well as ethnic origin, gender and sexuality.
- There is a very sound business case for diversity, taking into account demographic trends, availability of skills and the benefits that will be gained from employing a richer, more diverse workforce.
- There is also a sound ethical case for responding to diversity.
- The need for organizations to tackle diversity issues is highlighted by the extensive legislation, such as the Race Relations (Amendment) Act, the Sex Discrimination Act and the Human Rights Act, and the legal requirement for government organizations to take affirmative action in a number of areas.
- We invited you to examine the impact of globalization and how this could affect your own diversity strategies. In particular we looked at the global reach of UK companies and the ways in which some UK industries are having to look outside the United Kingdom to find suitably skilled workers.
- We noted the importance of devising diversity policies. However, we emphasized the need to ensure that such policies are implemented and translated into action. In this regard we suggested that structured programme and project management was essential.

NOTES

1 Discrimination on the grounds of nationality is dealt with elsewhere in the Treaty.
2 Unless the employer is able to show good reason. Employers would not be expected to make any changes to existing practice which would contravene health or safety legislation.
3 There are a number of exceptions such as health and safety issues.

Chapter 3

Learning to Learn About Diversity

By the time you have worked through this chapter we hope that you will have:

- explored the question of whether diversity is essentially a training or an education issue;
- considered the implications of learning about diversity for the learner and for the organization;
- identified the key components of a model of 'good' diversity training, and thought through how you might use this in your own context;
- understood the concept of 'opening up variation' for the learner and identified some examples of ways that this can happen;
- been introduced to the idea of using minority groups in training, and how this relates to opening up variation for the learner.

DIVERSITY: TRAINING OR EDUCATION?

Diversity training has become a pervasive element in many organizational training programmes. In Chapter 2 we outlined the business case for diversity and the way many organizations are responding to this. In the past few years there have been a number of key drivers which have generated the need for what has become known as 'diversity awareness' or 'community and race relations' or 'race awareness' training. We discussed examples of those drivers in Chapter 2. They include:

- The Race Relations (Amendment) Act 2000;
- *The Stephen Lawrence Inquiry* report;
- the Modernizing Government programme.

In thinking about how we learn about issues of diversity, there are a number of factors that need to be developed. There is an important issue around what is meant by 'awareness', since very often the claim that is made for training is that the intention is to raise people's awareness of something. This, of course, assumes a number of things about awareness which cannot, or at least should not, be overlooked. For example, we need to know what 'awareness' is commonly taken to mean. More importantly, if someone's awareness of something is raised, in what sense can he or she be said to have learnt something? If 'awareness' is assumed to be a lower level objective than the person being able to do something, or think about something, then in what sense can awareness have anything to do with training at all?

For the time being let us concentrate on the way diversity training sits in relationship to education and training. The question is an important one because it addresses issues of processes and outcomes. This is important because if we talk about 'diversity training' when we really mean 'diversity education', there is potentially a huge difference between the way we will do it and the expectations we have of it.

What do we mean by processes and outcomes? Essentially it is that the assumed processes and outcomes of education and training are often quite different. Spinks and Clements (1993: 20) charted some 'educational opposites' that may be identified between education and training. Compare some of the opposites in Figure 3.1 with your thinking so far about where diversity sits.

Education	Training
Learner-centred	Teacher-centred
Freedom	Authority
Process	Product
Facilitative	Didactic
Person-centred	Task-centred
Wholeness	Fragmentation
Syllabus-free	Syllabus-bound
Interconnected	Linear
Divergent thinking	Convergent thinking
Experience-based	Information-based

Figure 3.1   *Education and training: some opposites*

The education and training opposites outlined in the figure suggest that, in their pure forms, education and training are quite different. The stress does need to be on the 'pure' here, because in reality education and training blend far more than this suggests. Having said that, it is important to think about where we stand on the issue of the extent to which this is education or training. We suggest a number of reasons why this is the case:

- It will influence the choice of methods for learning.
- The expected/anticipated benefits of the training will be better articulated.
- It will influence the bid for the time and money that need to be put into the programme if it is to be effective.
- It will recognize the complexity and emotional nature of the learning.
- It will influence the way the programme is evaluated and what it is reasonable to expect it to achieve.
- It will recognize that people are free to think for themselves and make their own choices.

A final point to make is that although, as you may have gathered, our own approach is that diversity is more something about which people should be educated than something they can be trained in, the reality is that in many organizations it is referred to as 'diversity training'. In order to facilitate communication we refer to 'diversity training' throughout this book. We use that phrase given the understanding that we also take it to include processes and outcomes that are more to do with an educational paradigm than a training one.

LEARNING IN THE DIVERSITY CONTEXT

In the introduction to the book we briefly looked at why diversity training is often considered 'special'. In this section we will develop those themes a little and relate them to the notion of learning to learn about diversity. It is well established in education and training circles that different people have different learning styles and preferences. For example, Honey and Mumford (1986) delineate learning styles such as activist, pragmatist, theorist and reflector. You may also have come across other descriptions of learners' preferences such as serialists/holists, where some learn by seeing the big picture first and others prefer to take things step by step.

Just as learners seem to have different styles and approaches to their learning, so it is equally being established that different learners handle the learning of different objects of learning in different ways. This arises out of the way in which a given learner experiences the phenomenon. So, for example, if we take a typical problem of mathematics and study the ways different learners go about tackling it, we will find that there is a limited and definable number of ways in which people go about solving the problem, because they are experiencing the problem in different ways. It is not a matter of rocket science: our own experience of diversity training (by which we are including the entire process from needs analysis through to evaluation) is that people most definitely experience the issue from different perspectives and in different ways. There seems to be a spectrum of both experience and world-view. This ranges from the overt racist/discriminator who views diversity as an affront to racial or cultural purity (thankfully such people are rare) to those who seem to be role models for how to embrace a diverse society and celebrate it.

Pause for reflection

Consider each of the statements below. How do they relate to your own experience of learning? How do they relate to any experience you may have of learning about diversity?

- Diversity education/training needs to take account of the potential for learners to have a preferred learning style.
- If we take any aspect of diversity – we want people to learn, for example, the impact of institutional racism – we need to recognize that people will handle that learning in different ways.

A MODEL FOR 'GOOD' DIVERSITY TRAINING

Clements (2000) proposed a model of 'good' equal opportunities training which was grounded in research into the experience of trainers engaging in delivering equal opportunities, community and race relations, and other courses with different titles but essentially about fair treatment. It is our experience that the model can equally be applied to what has become known as diversity training. Essentially the model has four components. These are shown in Figure 3.2.

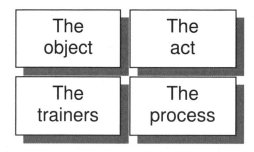

Figure 3.2   *A model of 'good' equal opportunities training*
Source: Clements (2000)

The object of diversity training

Aims and objectives are a necessary component of training which conforms to the systems-based product model that predominates in training. They can sometimes give the illusion that there is clarity of purpose, when in fact they may create a dissonance between what is specified for trainers to achieve and what trainers believe they should be aiming at. Aims and objectives do have a role to play in helping to make training accountable to the many stake-holders in it, but they may not be entirely helpful to instructors or learners, where the processes and outcomes of training may not be so easy to express, certainly in pure behavioural terms.

In vocational training paid for out of training budgets, which in turn may be reliant on public funds, there must be a concern for accountability. This, however, should not get in the way of specifying training that works with learners at a deeper and more meaningful level than merely aiming at behavioural competencies. The notion of competence and quality in educa-tion has led to a focus on outcomes which has ignored at its peril ideas about how the process of learning a particular thing can affect that outcome.

Once this has been said, it is vitally important that trainers know what the object of diversity training is, or should be. Some vague idea of raised awareness is not sufficient. Figure 3.3 helps to focus on what the objects of good diversity training should be.

'Raising awareness', as we have already noted, appears as the object of many diversity training programmes. For this to be useful, however, it can only be regarded as an overarching object for learning that goes much deeper. Such learning is represented by an increased knowledge that has both an internal and an external dimension to it. For people's awareness to

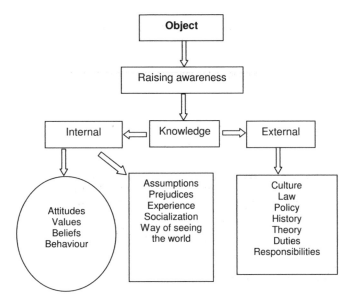

Figure 3.3   *The objects of good diversity training*

be truly raised they will need to increase their knowledge of themselves as well as knowledge of things outside of themselves, and sometimes outside of their own experience of life.

To respond properly to a diversity training agenda, learners will need to be able to get in touch with their own attitudes, values and beliefs – what they are, and where they come from. This self-knowledge will lead to an examination of their own assumptions, prejudices and so on (see Figure 3.3). A crucial aspect of this self-knowledge will be learners getting in touch with their way of seeing the world. To gain an understanding of one's world-view, which in itself is bound into attitudes, values and beliefs, will be the key to recognizing and valuing the fact that others' world-view may be different. This, it seems to us, lies at the very core of being able to value diversity.

The act of diversity training

The act of diversity training is an element of the model that has its focus on what the learner is doing when he or she engages in such training. In other words it refers to how the learner is personally engaging in the process to achieve the objects. Figure 3.4 plots some of the key activities that learners engage in when they are learning about diversity.

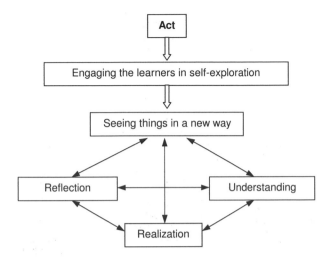

Figure 3.4   *Key activities in learning about diversity*

'Understanding', 'seeing things in a new way', 'reflection' and 'realization' are all key to facilitating the deeper level of self-exploration that is needed for effective learning around diversity. Let us take each of those in turn and examine it in a little more detail, in particular putting them in the context of learning to learn about diversity.

Understanding

Awareness was linked with knowledge above, but it is also strongly connected with understanding. Just to know things about diversity or to know things about oneself in relation to diversity is not enough. There needs to be meaning attached to this knowledge, and that is embodied in understanding.

Trainers and educators often express the search for 'meaning' in terms of visual metaphors such 'looking into' that which is being learned or 'looking at' it in the sense of seeing that which is being learned as a whole, or gaining 'insight' into the situation, or 'examining things'. Such visual metaphors are helpful because they enable us to take a number of perspectives on how learners go about understanding diversity.

Seeing things in a new way

Being able to see things in new ways is very important because we need to recognize that others may see the world quite differently from the way we see it. As we identified above, their way of experiencing a certain aspect of the world might be quite different from ours. The assumptions we hold tend to be built upon our own way of experiencing, and therefore in diversity training all our assumptions need to be challenged. We need not necessarily actually come to see the world differently, but we need certainly to reach a point of realization that others might, and that those other ways of seeing are equally as valid as our own.

Coming to see the world differently, and having our assumptions challenged, are very likely to be uncomfortable, even painful, processes, and this needs to be taken account of in a model of good diversity training. This is particularly so in terms of the trainer's ability to create a learning environment where it is safe for the learner to take risks in his or her learning. Coming to see things in a different way may or may not be a sudden experience for the learner, but however it happens, a process of exploration will precede it, and this exploration will involve an element of increased self-knowledge.

Reflection

Another crucial component of learning diversity is reflection. This immediately raises a question of semantics, since the word 'reflection' can be understood in several ways. For example there is the 'reflective practitioner' described by Schön (1983), as well as other ways in which 'reflection' can be used variously to mean 'reflect back' in the sense of mirror, 'think about', 'dwell on' or think about in a way that leads to some change. The last two are most prevalent, and in addition there are some qualities of reflection that are useful for the model.

- There is a range of objects for reflection on the part of learners.
- Reflection can only happen effectively as a voluntary act on the part of the learner.
- Reflection may happen during, immediately after or some time after the training event.

Realization

Truthful and honest reflection on the part of the learner may result in him or her becoming 'consciously aware'. This is often expressed by trainers as an act of 'realization'. The outcome of realization is also expressed as a state of 'heightened awareness'. The timing of realization runs in parallel to the act of reflection described above. Realization may happen suddenly in the context of a classroom session, where for some this will be like a light switching on and may be connected with experiencing a new way of seeing something. There are some parallels here with gestalt psychology and 'aha' moments, or the achievement of *pragnanz*, or meaningfulness (Hill, 1985), and the idea of focal awareness (Marton and Booth, 1997).

Although realization is often sudden, it may be the result of a period of reflection which might take place during the day of the training, overnight or even over a longer period. This is an important point for the model, since some trainers may have unreal expectations of what they can achieve in a short time, and may not take into account the power of reflection on the part of the learner. A final point for the model in relation to realization is that in connection with 'heightened awareness' there may be dissonance set up for the learner. This is because learners might discover aspects of their lives that they are not happy with, and it is likely that this will be an uncomfortable experience. This leads us on in the construction of the model to the penultimate element, the process, which of necessity includes some statements about the discomfort and pain that may be involved.

The process of diversity training

The process of diversity training is an element of the model that relates to either the conditions under which the training is taking place or some qualitative aspect of it. So this element includes issues about authority to engage with the learners at other than merely a cognitive level, and the way in which diversity training is likely to involve an element of discomfort or pain for the learner (and sometimes the trainer). Several trainers describe the process in terms of being on a journey.

Some trainers work in the firm belief that they are mandated by their organization to challenge learners and take them into areas where they may feel uncomfortable. An alternative view is that if a learner does not want to take part in the process then the trainer has to accept that. A further way of seeing the problem is that trainers feel that they want to engage with learners in a way that challenges them to explore their attitudes, values and beliefs because they know this makes for effective diversity training, but they are reluctant to do so because they do not feel they have either organizational sanction or the moral right to do it.

It seems to us that a model of good diversity training cannot embody all three approaches. Given what has been built up so far in terms of the object and act of diversity training, it becomes apparent that to adopt a position which expresses reluctance to engage with learners is to approach the training from a standpoint which is unlikely to succeed. Trainers need to be clear that they are mandated by the organization to deliver this training, that organizational values embody the expectation that the employees will share in them, and that learners who are unwilling to engage in the process are effectively distancing themselves from the values.

A model of good diversity training will recognize that when people engage in an exploration of their attitudes, values, beliefs and prejudices, this may be an uncomfortable process. Some will find out things about themselves that will cause them emotional pain, and often the tension in learners will relate to how they should respond. This discomfort may be a necessary factor in personal growth in diversity training terms, and rather than shy away from it or try to avoid it, the process should be constructed in a way that enables the discomfort to take place in a secure and supportive environment. This will involve skill on the part of the trainer, and carefully thought through issues of confidentiality and group contract. Trainers need to recognize that the ways in which some learners respond to discomfort include discrediting the course, avoiding the process, and retreating into a safety-net/comfort zone. Ironically these might be taken as an indicator of a successful process, and that the person is being challenged effectively.

The analogy of the journey is one frequently used by trainers to describe the overall process of diversity training. It is a powerful one and has a number of qualities. The analogy stresses, for example, the need for the training to be learner centred, in the sense that each person's journey will be an individual one and will have a different starting point. The learner must complete the journey in a model of good diversity training. So it would not be good training to exit just at the point of increased knowledge. Learners need to go further in a process of self-exploration to achieve the objects in the first element, such as understanding, and seeing the world in different ways so that they feel they can sit comfortably with the purpose and values of the organization. Through reflection, realization and understanding, the journey will be one of exploration. Things will be discovered that might not have been planned for, and each person will experience the exploration in a different way. A successful outcome of the journey is one where the student has been empowered to make his or her own choices, which are congruent with the values of the organization.

Being on a journey with the trainer may have the effect of making the training less threatening, and will help to engage the learner's interest. The journey should be made in the context of the individual's life experience. The trainers can act in the role of guide and will have metaphorically

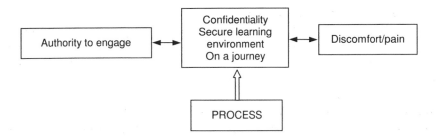

Figure 3.5　*The process of diversity training*

gathered together the equipment needed for a journey of exploration. Figure 3.5 gathers all these strands together in diagrammatic form.

The trainers who engage in diversity training

The final element of our model includes themes about the trainers themselves. This includes the skills that diversity trainers need, and their own knowledge, understanding and acceptance of the issues. The skills and attributes needed by trainers can be identified, and these are summarized in Table 3.1.

The skills and attributes shown in the table are those identified by trainers in the research on which the model we are describing is based (Clements, 2000). Look at each in turn and make an honest assessment of whether you have the skills and attributes needed to be an effective diversity trainer. Do you have skills and attributes that are not in the list? How do they make you more effective? Do you need to develop in any of the areas? How could you achieve that?

Trainers need to be able to facilitate effectively because they need to work with learners at a level that is much more than one of knowledge transmission. They have to be clear about what they are trying to do and how they will do it, but at the same time they need to be flexible to adapt to changing circumstances in the classroom. Trainers who do not have the appropriate skill to work in sensitive and emotional areas may actually cause psychological damage to learners. They should not engage in diversity training until they have identified their own prejudices, worked through their own positions in relation to diversity issues, and had their own attitudes exposed. This is important for a number of reasons.

Table 3.1 *Skills and attributes needed by trainers*

Skills	Attributes
Intervention	Resilience ('take it on the chin')
Facilitation	Belief in what you are doing
Conflict management	Mental agility
Asking tough questions	Deep understanding of issues
Flexibility	Positive outlook
Managing group dynamics	Recognize own limits
Knowledge of law	Been through the process
Managing resistance strategies	Sincerity
Knowledge of policy issues	Sensitive to people's needs and concerns
Knowledge of own prejudice	Non-neutral in facilitation
Knowledge of own attitudes, values and beliefs	'Walk the talk'/'Own the ethos'
	Motivation in the subject
	Well trained in diversity

- First, they need to be sincere and committed to what they are doing, and need to know how they personally respond to the issues around which they will be facilitating.
- Second, they need to have attitudes, values, beliefs and behaviour that are congruent with the subject of the training, and therefore also need to have had the opportunity to work through the areas of difficulty for them as individuals.
- Third, they need to recognize that if they are to engage in this type of training, stress can be a problem. This can range from feeling devalued to feeling that they are not getting anywhere. Some classroom situations will be very emotionally charged and challenging to deal with, and they need to be able to cope with such situations. Working at a level which is effective will involve the discomfort, pain and even trauma that self-exploration can involve. To deal with this, the trainer needs to be not only a skilled facilitator, but also resilient, sensitive, flexible, able to read body language, skilled in recognizing and responding to group dynamics and confident to lead learners on a journey which may be difficult.

Diversity trainers may find they suffer stress quite unlike the stresses involved in training other topics. One of the solutions to this stress is to have a support mechanism for trainers, and the model should include this. Support staff trainers may have particular problems, which according to the data may range from their credibility being challenged through to actual experiences of being bullied. We deal with this more fully as an issue in Chapter 6. Figure 3.6 draws these strands together.

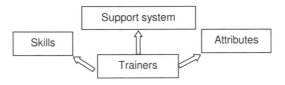

Figure 3.6   *Support for trainers*

An experientially derived model of diversity training

Figure 3.7 shows the four components of the model of good diversity training laid out together. It represents the way in which trainers experience diversity training.

An important dimension of learning to learn about diversity is the way trainers see and experience their role. A number of studies have revealed differences in teachers' ways of experiencing teaching. Prosser and Trigwell (1997: 246), for example, identified different conceptions of the teaching role shown in Table 3.2. Look at the conceptions and compare them with your own conception of teaching. What implications might your conception have for diversity training? Which conception might be the most powerful for effective teaching and learning of diversity?

OPENING UP VARIATION FOR THE LEARNER

There has been a great deal of research in recent years which indicates that the key way in which we learn things is through being able to discern variation. We see this as making a significant contribution to how learners may learn about diversity. Marton and Booth (1997), who have been in the forefront of this research, give an interesting example of how this works. Suppose you are in a forest in which there are deer. The light is fading and there are dark trees and bushes in which a deer is standing. In order to see the deer you need to discern its outline and contours from the background against which it stands. In order to do this you need to be able to recognize

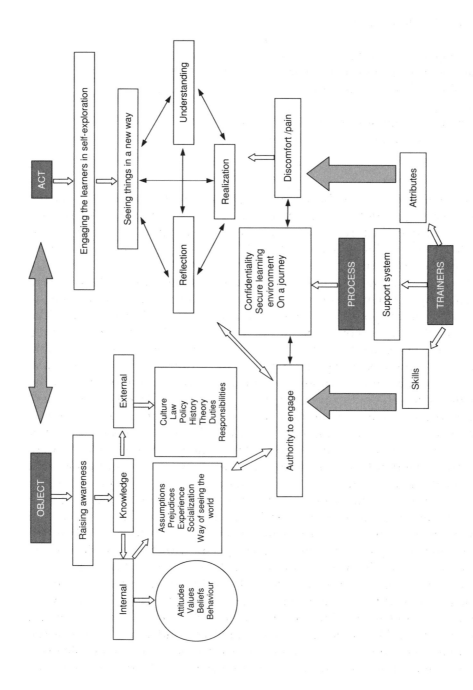

Figure 3.7 *A model of good diversity training*

Table 3.2   *How teaching is seen*

Teaching as transmitting concepts of the syllabus
Teaching as transmitting teachers' knowledge
Teaching as helping students acquire concepts of the syllabus
Teaching as helping students acquire teachers' knowledge
Teaching as helping students develop conceptions
Teaching as helping students change conceptions

it as a deer – you need to be able to assign meaning to what you are seeing. That meaning needs to be separated out from its context – otherwise you will not see the deer, just trees and bushes. Without variation in the context you would never be able to see the deer. Without meaning you would never discern the variation.

Another example of variation helps to make the point in perhaps a more striking way. Bowden and Marton (1998: 34) give an example drawn from the work of an anthropologist who visited a small remote village in Turkey. The water of the village contained a type of bacteria which to the observing anthropologist seemed to cause the people of the village a stomach problem. Everyone in the village experienced the same problem, since they all drank the same water, and the condition remained throughout their lives in the village. When the anthropologist interviewed the villagers no one mentioned the stomach problem they seemed to have. Because everyone was experiencing the same thing in the same way the stomach disorder did not represent any variation from the norm. The result was that the villagers were not aware that they had a stomach disorder which was caused by the bacteria.

Now think about diversity from a similar perspective. One of the key points that we have made in this chapter is that people have different ways of seeing and experiencing the world in which they live. Many people, and in particular in this country the white majority, tend only to be able to see the world from a particular white majority perspective. So the world appears to be one where whiteness is assumed. If the possibility of diversity is not taken into account, then for people in the white majority it is very easy to package the world they see in such a way that it effectively excludes other possibilities. In Chapter 6 we discuss the notion of institutional racism and discrimination. We would argue that one of the underlying causes of the phenomenon of institutional racism and discrimination is that people make majority assumptions and never properly engage with the reality that in fact we live in a diverse society. Not all people share the assumptions that are made by a white majority.

One of the aims of diversity training then needs to be to open up variation for the learner. In this way a diversity trainer will empower learners to discern variation in a whole range of ways including:

- variation in people's life experience;
- variation in culture;
- variation in value systems;
- variation in beliefs;
- variation in what can be assumed.

A practical way of achieving such variation is to involve people from minority groups in the training process. By giving first-hand accounts of the way they experience and see the world, they can open up variation for the learners. This leads us to consider how in reality we might do this.

INVOLVING MINORITY GROUPS IN YOUR TRAINING

The Stephen Lawrence Inquiry report recommended for the police service:

> That police training and practical experience in the field of racism awareness and valuing cultural diversity should regularly be conducted at local level. And that it should be recognized that local minority ethnic communities should be involved in such training and experience.

> (Macpherson, 1999: 332, recommendation 50)

For the police this represented a major change in the way that training in diversity issues is addressed. In fact the trend has been to broaden the remit to try to involve minority perspectives in all aspects of training, from needs analysis through design to delivery and evaluation. Involving various communities in all aspects of training is an essential component of learning to learn about diversity. For too long majority groups both set the agenda for training and held on to the power in terms of evaluating its effectiveness. In learning to learn about diversity, there must be a concern to be inclusive rather than exclusive in all aspects of training.

Pause for reflection

As one who is interested in developing diversity in your own context, reflect on all the reasons why you might want to involve minority groups in your training programmes. What groups would you want to involve? What would the issues be in terms of how you might involve them?

The importance of involving communities in diversity training

We can summarize the importance and value of involving others in training as follows:

- Diversity is essentially about the recognition of the difference between people, groups of people and communities. If the training agenda is to be properly reflective of that difference, then others need to be involved in its development.
- Involving diverse groups in developing and delivering training will bring other world-views to it which could not otherwise be reflected.
- If the aim is to 'open up variation' for the learner, then the first-hand experience of someone from a minority community will be much more powerful than reported experience.
- Learning will be enriched through shared experience.
- Minority groups gain a sense of being included, rather than excluded, and will be able to express the issues as they are experienced by them rather than how someone else believes they are experienced.

In the pause for reflection activity above we asked you to consider what groups you might want to involve in developing and delivering a diversity programme and what issues this might raise. There are a number of factors that need to be taken into account.

What is a community?

There are several ways in which we might understand the term 'community'.

Communities may just mean neighbourhoods, or where people live. Their sense of community may come from simply being located together. Very often this is more noticeable where the numbers of people are smaller, such as in small towns or villages, maybe in rural settings. In urban areas the sense of community in a neighbourhood may be completely absent or may be restricted to groups of houses or flats. This is important because in involving the community it is important to establish that people who speak for a neighbourhood community might in fact be speaking for a very small number of people. Their experience is, of course, perfectly valid, but you need to take care that a range of views are represented.

Communities can also comprise people who, while not living in the same neighbourhood, have a community of interest. So we often hear the phrase 'the business community' where what is being referred to is the unifying interest that individuals have in a particular area of business. Again, this is important as for many organizations there is a need to identify the communities of interest that they serve in order to meet their diverse needs properly.

The third and possibly most powerful way of thinking about community is where there is a community of identity. This does not depend on where people live, neither does it depend on a particular interest, but it is defined by the way people see themselves. This leads to a much broader way of thinking about diversity. Communities of identity may include for example:

- young people;
- people from ethnic minority backgrounds;
- people who are gay, lesbians, bisexual or transgender;
- asylum seekers and refugees;
- people who identify themselves in terms of their religion or faith, such as Muslims, Jewish people, Christians, Hindus, Sikhs and so on;
- Gypsies, travellers and Roma.

An important point to note in regard to all of the above is that many people identify with more than one community. The practical outcome of this is that we need to take care not to assign people to a particular group in a stereotypical way, and then make the assumption that that is all there is to say about them, or more importantly that this is the way they would identify themselves.

Pause for reflection

Think about what we have been saying about communities. What communities do you identify with? What does this say about you and the way you see the world? How might it be different for others?

Many agencies who engage in diversity training programmes routinely involve communities in all aspects of their training to maximize its impact and open up variation for learners. We are grateful to Dianna Yach of Ionann management consultants for the contribution of elements of good practice in community involvement depicted in Figure 3.8.

A final point to note is that diversity training and diversity programmes generally will be considerably empowered by the proper involvement of diverse communities. This may also include involving communities with your organization.

We close this section with a short poem which was written by a black community contributor to some community and race relations (CRR) training for a group of senior managers. He wrote it spontaneously to express

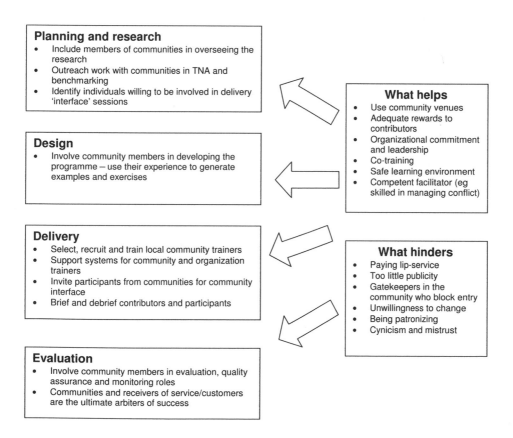

Figure 3.8   *Good practice in involving the community in diversity training*

what he was feeling during a plenary feedback session with the managers. We think it perfectly captures what we have been trying to say.

> We are hard at work everyday, trying to make changes – that's the key.
> Not first for me or you, but changes for the future,
> That's what we all want to see,
> A better tomorrow, for you and me,
> Whether we're black, white, pink or yellow
> Challenging the way we work, the way we think, and de things that we do
> At work for me and you.
> No matter what department you work in –
> CRR is a very important key,
> Just like health and safety.
> So smile, and take on board CRR
> JAH LOVE it's that easy. . .
> (Reproduced with kind permission of Charles Carrington, community contributor from Reading)

KEY LEARNING POINTS

In this chapter we have taken a theoretical view of learning to learn about diversity. Later in the book we will present a practical application of the theory.

- Our point of departure was to consider where diversity training sits in relation to education and training. We noted that many of the aims and processes involved in diversity are actually oriented more towards education than training.
- Drawing on research that was conducted among trainers engaged in the field of equal opportunities, race awareness and diversity, we examined the components of a model of good diversity training. The complete model, which has four main parts, was presented as Figure 3.7. We argued that 'good' diversity training will address all the components of the model.
- The first component of the model challenged thinking about the object of this type of training. 'Awareness' involves knowledge of self as well as knowledge of the issues.

- The act of diversity training was presented as having four key elements for learning: understanding, seeing things in a new way, reflection and realization.
- The process of diversity training needs to take account of creating a secure learning environment and is analogous to taking the learner on a journey.
- The trainers engaging in this type of training need the appropriate skills and attributes, and will need support to cope with the stress that they will experience.
- Effective application of the model will be to a certain extent dependent on the trainers' view of teaching and learning. There was an opportunity to consider your own conception of teaching.
- We looked at the theory of variation as a way of understanding how people learn, and considered ways of opening up variation for learners.
- Finally we considered involving minority communities in diversity programmes, the importance of this for variation, and examples of what constitutes good practice.

Chapter 4

A Knowledge Base for Diversity Training

Knowledge – that is, education in its true sense – is our best protection against unreasoning prejudice and panic-making fear, whether engendered by special interest, illiberal minorities, or panic-stricken leaders.

Franklin D Roosevelt

LEARNING INTENTIONS

On completing this chapter we hope that you will have:

- developed an understanding of a range of psychological theories of human thought processes and behaviours which impact on the concept of diversity;
- considered the concepts of racism, sexism, homophobia and issues surrounding disability;
- examined some commonly used models used to define the relationship between attitudes and behaviour and responses to dominance.

INTRODUCTION

The purpose of this chapter is to provide you with a knowledge base with regard to some of the underlying features of diversity training. Each of the sub-headings of this chapter is probably the subject of a book in its own right. We will not, therefore, provide a detailed analysis. Rather we will outline the key features and provide you with references so that you can undertake more detailed research as appropriate. The scope of this book also prevents us from addressing all of the issues, definitions, concepts, notions and theories. We have therefore included those areas that are most commonly addressed in diversity training.

We have worked with a number of trainers who have found the concept of attitudes, values, beliefs and the interrelationship with behaviour initially difficult to grasp. This is unsurprising as the area is both complex and challenging, and remains a constant source of research and debate for psychologists. However, we feel that it is important to develop some degree of understanding of the various definitions for a number of reasons.

First, there have been a number of occasions when we have worked with sponsors of training events who are themselves confused about the terms and have an unrealistic expectation of what the training event can actually achieve. One sponsor in particular was disappointed to learn that the three-day awareness course he had commissioned was unlikely to result in whole-sale attitudinal change.

Second, it is important that you develop an understanding of your responsibilities and boundaries as a diversity trainer; in our work as trainer trainers we have frequently found newly trained trainers who have taken on the mantle of quasi-psychotherapists wanting to drill down into the process of the learning event at the expense of the content.

Finally, diversity training is challenging; it confronts individuals' attitudes, values and beliefs; very often you will be required to challenge inappropriate language and behaviour, and you may also be challenged by your delegates. This can take the form of non-participation throughout the training or, in some cases, an outright challenge to what you have said.

The scope of this chapter is summarized in Figure 4.1.

ATTITUDES

If the sponsors of training are confused by some of the terms, they are not helped by some of the many competing and, in some cases, contradictory definitions of 'attitudes'. Reber and Reber, authors of *The Penguin Dictionary of Psychology* (2001), state that attitude comprises the following components:

- cognitive (a consciously held belief or opinion);
- affective (emotions, mood and feeling);

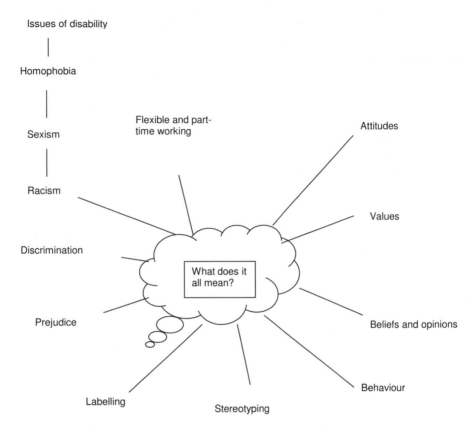

Figure 4.1   *The scope of the chapter*

- evaluative (to determine the negative or positive value of something);
- conative: an ordered arrangement of elements (such as stereotypes) which are likely to lead to a particular behaviour.

From a research perspective Clark and Miller (1970) describe an attitude as:

> a disposition, acquired through previous experience, to react to certain things, people or events in positive ways. Attitudes represent a tendency to approach or avoid that which maintains or threatens the things one values. Like the values from which they are often derived, attitudes have an effect upon and are consistently related to beliefs and behaviour.

Attitudes can be developed by individuals, by small groups, by communities and by populations. A commonly held attitude within a group can develop a group culture. Attitudes develop over time and can change according to different circumstances. They are hypothetical constructs: in other words they are not themselves observable. However, they are manifest in behaviours such as speech, writing, non-verbal communication and physical behaviours.

We are frequently asked whether attitudes can be changed. The simple and somewhat glib answer is of course yes; however, the process of changing attitudes can be time consuming and requires sophisticated processes.

Generational attitude change

Attitude surveys are frequently used to monitor attitude changes over time, and it is widely accepted that attitudes towards a number of areas changed during the 20th century. In this way the attitudes of one generation can be compared with another.

One option is to compare modern and post-modern attitudes. In this regard modernist attitudes (also known as materialist) are those attitudes which emerged in the 19th and early 20th centuries; post-modernist attitudes (post-materialist) have emerged in the developed world since the Second World War. The Local Government Association (2000) outlined some key differences between modern and post-modern attitudes, which are shown in Table 4.1.

In another example, in the United States research looked at the attitudinal differences between different generations using the following categories:

- Baby Boom generation – those born between 1943 and 1960;
- 13th generation – those born between 1961 and 1982;
- Millennium generation – those who have been and were expected to be born between 1982 and 2003.

Five historical events and activities that occurred during the formative years of 13th-generation individuals were said to be responsible for shaping their attitudes. These were:

- the information explosion;
- technological advances;
- economics;
- political changes;
- scientific advances.

Table 4.1   *Modern and post-modern attitudes*

Modern/materialist	Post-modern/post-materialist
Increased wealth/economic growth	Wider quality of life issues
Deference and respect for legal authority	Challenges to status quo
Extended family and social obligations	Individual self-expression
Allegiance to large institutions (Church, trade unions, etc)	Individual value systems and increasing acceptance of and respect for social and cultural diversity
Hierarchy	Heterarchy
Male values of authority	Female values of authority

Source: Local Government Association (2000)

The same question was asked of a group from the Millennium generation. They identified the following events:

- the *Challenger* explosion;
- the ending of the Cold War;
- the first Gulf war;
- AIDS and other sexually transmitted diseases;
- the Rodney King incident in Los Angeles, USA.

Consider these two questions:

In your view what recent events are likely to shape the attitudes of younger members of society?
Do you think that these events will challenge the attitudes of those from a different generation?

Attitude change in groups

Generational attitude change is normally the result of large-scale significant events; attitudinal change in small groups is a different concept. National

Police Training (NPT, 2001) describes the three main approaches to changing attitude as:

- the power/coercive approach;
- the empirical/rational approach;
- the normative/re-educative approach.

The power/coercive approach

This approach is based on the premise that changing and/or adopting new behaviours will eventually lead to attitudinal change. It is more commonly known as behaviour modification or behaviour modelling. Typically the process comprises four distinct stages. First, specific measurable behavioural objectives are devised to describe in detail the new desired behaviour. This behaviour is demonstrated by a role model (such as a trainer) and then continually repeated by individuals within the group. Finally, feedback is provided as to whether or not the practised behaviour meets the objectives devised in the first stage.

The empirical/rational approach

This approach is quite simply the use of information that is intended to appeal to rational logic. It is quite often used as part of national government advertising campaigns such as road safety campaigns, anti-drink drive programmes and anti-smoking advertisements.

The normative/re-educative approach

This approach is frequently used in attitude change training. It uses a number of processes (described in more detail below) which encourage individuals to examine their own attitudes and expose them for review by others within the group. The peer group and group leaders then provide feedback (for example, regarding the appropriateness of the behaviour) which should be supportive and non-judgemental. Individuals are then encouraged to confront their attitudes.

Attitude change and diversity training

In our experience long-term and substantial attitudinal change is unlikely to occur as a result of short-term awareness training, which is typically concerned with increasing knowledge and understanding. In this regard we have

Table 4.2   *Bloom's taxonomy of learning*

Level	Skills
Knowledge	Observation and recall of information Knowledge of key data
Comprehension	Understanding of information Interpretation of data Comparison and contrasting of facts
Application	Uses information Utilizes models, theories and concepts when given new information Solves problems using information
Analysis	Recognizes patterns of information Recognizes hidden meanings Identifies separate components of the whole
Synthesis	Uses old information to create new ideas Uses information from various sources Predicts outcomes and draws conclusions
Evaluation	Compares and contrasts ideas Assesses value of theories Recognizes subjectivity

found Bloom's taxonomy of learning to be a useful framework to better understand the relationship between levels of learning and learning intentions (www.officeport.com/edu/blooms.htm). It is summarized in Table 4.2.

In our experience attitudinal change is one of the most difficult outcomes to achieve through the delivery of training. Very often diversity training will consist of one or two days of awareness training (at the level of knowledge and possibly comprehension) and attitudinal change is frequently beyond the scope of this sort of training event. Attitudinal change is more likely to occur as the result of longer-term educational programmes (which will move to the levels of synthesis or evaluation) or specially designed training programmes such as T groups or structured group learning in which the underlying attitudes, values, beliefs and assumptions are frequently challenged.

As was noted by Clark and Miller (see above), attitudes are closely linked with values, and it is to this area which we now turn.

VALUES

What are your values, and where do they originate? Try the exercise in Figure 4.2. Obviously there are no right and wrong answers, and any number of values may be seen as important. They might be wide-ranging principles such as freedom, justice or democracy. They might be traits such as honesty, loyalty or openness.

Figure 4.2 *Try to identify your own value system by identifying the 10 values that are most important to you*

Values in the sense of diversity training can be described as 'an abstract and general principle concerning the patterns of behaviour within a particular culture or society which, through a process of socialization, the members of that culture or society hold in high regard'. Often referred to as social values, they form the central principles which allow the integration of individual and societal values. However, there are obvious examples where societal values may clash with individual attitudes.

Think of three examples where there is a contradiction between a societal value and an individual attitude. Again there are many examples which you could have identified, and you might have included the following:

- a racist who is living in a democratic, developed country which is committed to the European Convention for Human Rights;
- a male manager who has consistently and over a long period of time treated women staff less favourably than male colleagues within an organization that is committed to equal opportunities;
- a homophobe who frequently attacks and assaults men and who frequents a public house known to be popular with homosexual men.

Individual values comprise a judgement about what is right, good or bad, and as with attitudes they can be shared by other members of a community, generation or population. Consider the values in Figure 4.3 that might differ between cultures, communities or individuals:

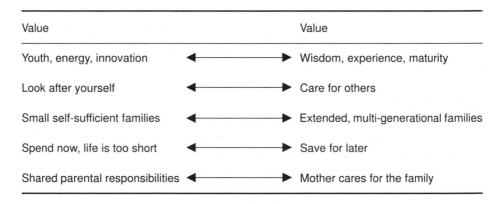

Value		Value
Youth, energy, innovation	◄──────►	Wisdom, experience, maturity
Look after yourself	◄──────►	Care for others
Small self-sufficient families	◄──────►	Extended, multi-generational families
Spend now, life is too short	◄──────►	Save for later
Shared parental responsibilities	◄──────►	Mother cares for the family

Figure 4.3   *Values that might differ between cultures, communities or individuals*

As we noted above, beliefs and opinions are closely associated with attitudes and values, and we will now look in more detail at how beliefs and opinions are formed.

BELIEFS AND OPINIONS

As we discussed above, attitudes and values are formed over time and, in some cases, over generations. Beliefs and opinions are more individualistic and generally develop over a shorter period of time.

A belief generally is an emotional process which involves the acknowledgement of a proposition, statement or other kind of information. There are, therefore, some intellectual processes involved in the development of beliefs. However, a belief is often based on a proposition, and the holder may not have the full intellectual knowledge required to prove its veracity. Beliefs can be placed in a hierarchy dependent on their relative degree of certainty: for example, it is argued that there is a difference between a conviction and an opinion.

An opinion is less factually based. It is often held on the basis of tentative information and is often described as 'a point of view'. It is therefore an internalized process, although a collection of opinions expressed within a given culture might reflect the values and attitudes of that culture.

Beliefs and opinions are often challenged, particularly when they are based on fairly tenuous information. The majority of awareness training is designed to dispel mistaken beliefs and opinions, and to make people more aware of factual information such as new legislation.

It is often recognized that behaviour results from the cognitive and internalized processes of attitudes, values, beliefs and opinions, and we will now examine behaviour in more detail.

BEHAVIOUR

Over decades behaviour has been the subject of extensive research by psychologists. It remains a central feature of continuing psychological research, and there are many contradictory views as to what constitutes behaviour. At one end of the scale is the behaviourist view which regards behaviour as a series of overtly observable reflex actions, while others are of the view that there is a much closer and intricate relationship between internal, covert and mental processes and overt behaviour.

Why is it so important that we, as diversity trainers, understand the relationship between the mind and behaviour? Quite simply, discrimination is a behaviour involving the unequal treatment of a person because of that person's background or characteristics. Training is a means of changing behaviour, whether the desired change is improved workplace performance or the reduction of inappropriate language.

In Chapter 5 we outline the importance of setting out learning intentions as part of the design stage of diversity training. Some of these learning intentions will include specific behaviour-related objectives, and others may involve cognitive processes.

Any link between attitudes and behaviours has been, and remains, the subject of much heated debate among psychologists. Attitudes have been found to have a biasing effect on judgements. For example Munro and Ditto (1997) found that people were likely to view research that was consistent with their views on homosexuality as more convincing than research that was inconsistent with their views. A number of studies found that people who held strong views about particular subjects (for example environmental issues) were more likely than others to behave in ways that supported their attitude (say, by explaining to others the benefits from recycling waste). However other cognitive processes such as evaluation and judgement will determine whether the attitude is consistently expressed as an observable behaviour. Additional cognitive processes that may contribute in this regard include stereotyping, labelling and prejudice, and we will look at these areas in closer detail.

STEREOTYPING

'Stereotype' is derived from *stereos* (= rigid) and *tupos* (= trace). Lippman (1922) defined a stereotype as a 'picture in our heads'. Before we look at stereotypes in greater detail, use Figure 4.4 to record five strengths and five weaknesses of stereotyping.

Strengths	Weaknesses
1.	1.
2.	2.
3.	3.
4.	4.
5.	5.

Figure 4.4   *Strengths and weaknesses of stereotyping*

The term 'stereotyping' was originally used in the field of printing, where it referred to a solid plate or mould which would be difficult to recast once it had been cast. The term is now commonly used in social science as a means of describing a generalized view of a person or group of people, in which that view is typically:

- rigid;
- simplistic;

- overgeneralized;
- typically negative or unfavourable (although sometimes stereotypes can include positive but biased and inaccurate beliefs, eg all women make good mothers).

A definition of stereotyping which is gaining credibility with the world of social psychology is that stereotyping is a series of widely shared generalizations about the characteristics of a group or class of people (Reber and Reber, 2001). Reber and Reber argue that this more neutral definition is preferred as it:

- enables stereotypes to change;
- allows stereotypes which are both positive and accurate;
- highlights how stereotypes can be widely shared.

The more negatively biased first definition is generally the result of a process of labelling, and we will now examine this concept in more detail.

LABELLING

Labelling originated within the field of psychiatry to denote behaviour patterns which are generally seen as abnormal or unacceptable. As with the initial definition of stereotyping, it is seen as having negative connotations, particularly as there is a view that an individual who has been labelled is expected to exhibit behaviours that are consistent with the label. This can lead to what is commonly known as a self-fulfilling prophecy.

In the field of diversity training we often find that labelling and stereotyping behaviours are intrinsically linked. They often result from the notion of prejudice which we will now examine.

PREJUDICE

For Reber and Reber (2001), prejudice has three distinct definitions:

- It consists of an attitude that has been formed as a result of inaccurate or incomplete information. In other words it is a prejudgement or preconception. This is a rather literal definition, and one that allows for both negative and positive prejudices about anything.

- The second definition is more often used in the field of diversity training; it can be described as a negative attitude towards a particular group of persons which is the direct result of negative traits or images that are assumed to be attributable to all members of that group.
- The last definition is also commonly used within diversity training. This definition relates to a failure to treat a person as an individual who has specific and unique qualities. Rather it involves behaving towards people as if they have all of the presumed stereotypical qualities of the community or cultural group to which they belong.

As noted by Reber and Reber (2001), prejudice which falls within the last two definitions is frequently exhibited by members of a society's dominant group against members of the society's minority groups. Prejudice of this type is different from a preconception because of the cognitive processes which drive the type of prejudice described in the second and third definitions.

We have noted above the relationship between cognitive processes and behaviour, and the exhibition of behaviour such as discrimination is very often the result of prejudice.

DISCRIMINATION

Discrimination in the context of diversity is quite simply the demonstration of unequal treatment to an individual or group of persons on the basis of features such as their race, sexuality, gender, physical disposition or age.

Racism

The concept of 'race' was originally conceived within the field of anthropology, and was a very early, and now seen as misplaced, means of trying to distinguish between the different groups of human beings. The earliest attempts tried to define racial groups on the basis of characteristics such as hair texture, skin pigmentation and other physical characteristics. Obviously this is a highly contentious issue, particularly in respect of skin colour, where a person of mixed race, classified in this type of system as black, may have lighter skin than a person who is classified as white.

Reber and Reber (2001) note that the working definition of race is less one of genetic classification and increasingly one involving a wide range of social, cultural and political dimensions. Racism therefore can be described as a prejudice (see above) that is founded on the basis of race, in which other races are seen as inferior. Often racism is also used to describe racist behaviour.

Sexism

Very simply, sexism is a prejudice that is based on the gender of a person. However, the term is used interchangeably to describe both an attitude and belief that women are inferior, and any treatment or behaviour towards people which discriminates against them on the basis of their gender. Although the definition of sexism can apply to discriminatory behaviour or beliefs towards both sexes, the term 'sexism' is almost universally used to describe unequal treatment of women.

Homophobia

As with sexism, homophobia is used to describe both a cognitive process and an act or behaviour. In psychological terms phobia is used to describe a persistent fear or dread of a specific situation or stimulus (Reber and Reber, 2001). Literally, homophobia is the fear of homosexuals. However, as noted above, it can be used to describe any act of prejudice or discrimination expressed against homosexual people because of their sexuality. It is interesting to note that as recently as 1980 the American Psychiatric Association described homosexuality as a mental illness.

ISSUES OF DISABILITY

Consider the following. Six point five per cent of the UK population is disabled. Of these:

- a quarter of a million people have profound hearing loss;
- over one million are registered blind or partially sighted;
- 250,000 people have both visual and hearing impairment;
- almost the same numbers are admitted to hospital because of mental illness in England each year.

As we noted in Chapter 2, in certain circumstances, discriminating against someone because of his or her disability can be an offence against the Disability Discrimination Act, 1996. Since October 1999 service providers have had to consider making reasonable adjustments to the way they deliver their services so that disabled people are not prevented from accessing those services. From 2004 service providers have had to consider making perma-nent physical adjustments to their premises, such as providing ramps for wheelchair users.

The Disability Discrimination Act 1995 defines disability as a physical or mental impairment which has a substantial and long-term adverse effect on a person's ability to carry out normal day-to-day activities. This may include physical impairments affecting the senses, such as sight and hearing, and mental impairments, including learning disabilities and mental illness if recognized by a respected body of medical opinion. For an effect to be substantial, it must be classed as more than minor, such as an inability to see moving traffic clearly enough to cross a road safely or to remember and relay a simple message correctly. For the effects to be long term they must have lasted at least 12 months or are likely to last at least 12 months or are likely to last for the rest of the life of the person affected.

The Act also covers progressive conditions where impairments are likely to become substantial. Examples of progressive conditions include:

- cancer;
- HIV infection;
- multiple sclerosis;
- muscular dystrophy.

For more information visit the website www.drc-gb.org.

As with the Equal Pay Act and the Sex Discrimination Act, an important driver behind the existing and the proposed legislation is the desire to increase in the workplace the number of people from previously under-represented groups. Another policy intended to achieve this goal is to put into place more flexible working practices.

FLEXIBLE AND PART-TIME WORKING

There are many who believe that the notion of a Monday to Friday 9 am to 5 pm working week is a thing of the past. Part of this is due to the changing face of industry, the effects of globalization and the advent of technology. Those working in the finance industry are finding themselves having to take account of markets working in different time zones and having to start work earlier or finish work later. Technology such as mobile telephones, laptop computers and modems means that some office workers are no longer required to report to the office each and every day: more and more companies encourage home-based working which in turn can reduce operating overheads. However, it is arguably the increasing availability of part-time working that has had most impact in the workplace. The most important factor here is equality, so that part-time workers can enjoy, pro rata, the same benefits as their full-time colleagues.

KEY LEARNING POINTS

In this chapter we have outlined a number of theoretical concepts which we believe will have an importance in the management, design and delivery of diversity training.

- We noted a number of psychological theories of human thought processes and behaviours which impact on the concept of diversity. In particular we noted that attitudinal changes can occur over time and across generations. We highlighted the importance of encouraging the sponsors of learning to understand the limitations of what can be achieved, and we especially noted the misplaced perception that awareness training can result in attitudinal change.
- We considered the concepts of racism, sexism, homophobia and issues surrounding disability, and we outlined how in some cases (such as homophobia) the terminology can be used to describe both the attitude and the behaviour.

Chapter 5

Designing Diversity Training

By the time you have worked through this chapter we hope that you will have:

- identified the issues that need to be considered in conducting a needs analysis for diversity training;
- thought about how to differentiate aims, goals, learning intentions and objectives, and identified ways of writing them effectively;
- thought through the special implications of trying to achieve 'awareness' in diversity training;
- considered how you might use occupational standards in designing and delivering a diversity training programme;
- identified from examples, good practice in constructing and implementing a diversity training programme.

INTRODUCTION

Figure 5.1 represents the most basic form of a systematic approach to training. Over the years the experience of training managers, trainers and designers has been that the core elements shown of investigating the need, design, delivery and evaluation invariably must be present for a training programme to be effective. Having said that, many other models have been developed that are considerably more complicated. Generally this complication arises out of the complex nature of the core elements.

In this chapter we will concentrate on the first two elements of the model, namely investigating the need and designing the programme. This will be set firmly in the context of diversity. The remaining two elements, delivery and evaluation, each have a chapter devoted to them (Chapters 7 and 8

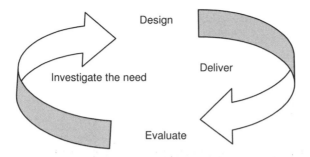

Figure 5.1 *Basic model of a systematic approach to training*

respectively). However, we are firmly of the opinion that evaluation should not be decoupled from the design of diversity training. It is essential from the outset to know, and be specific about, what the success of a programme would look like. In business terms this might be what business benefits we are expecting to accrue from the training. In public sector terms we might define success in terms of public satisfaction with a particular service, or organizational performance against certain criteria. Whatever the measure, it needs to be specified from the word go. Not only will this prevent the goalposts being moved to suit the outcomes – which is dishonest – it will also help to inform the design process.

NEEDS ANALYSIS

Before any work can begin on designing a diversity training programme, we need to be clear what the need is. Figure 5.2 shows a number of factors that will impinge on this stage of the design. It is vital to work through this stage first, since it is not uncommon to discover from the research that the problem is not a training problem at all, or at least not a problem that can be solved by training. Very often when things go wrong the easiest thing to hold responsible is training or the lack of it.

If it were true that institutional racism and discrimination were merely the result of a lack of training, then the solution to these would be relatively simple. In reality, there are many reasons why discrimination and racism persist – and for some of these training would make no difference. So we need to be clear that we are dealing with a problem that can be fixed by training. The needs analysis may, as a by-product, uncover things that could be put right in other ways, for example greater organizational flexibility,

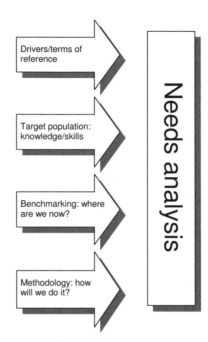

Figure 5.2   *Factors impinging on needs analysis*

changes to work practices, better quality assurance, better management or more robust policies.

Returning to Figure 5.2, let us look at the impinging factors in a little more detail. Before we do so it is worth noting an assumption we are making at this stage. We are assuming that you have picked up on the message in Chapter 3 that an essential ingredient to good diversity training is to involve communities, particularly minority communities, in all aspects of the needs analysis, design, delivery and evaluation of training. In this chapter we are taking that as a given.

Drivers/terms of reference

Most diversity training will take place as the result of one or more drivers, and there will be terms of reference for such training. Very often the driver will be something external to the organization. For example, the Modernizing Government initiative (HM Government, 2000) has led many government departments to take stock of their working practices. A key commitment within Modernizing Government is valuing public service.

Valuing public service

> A programme to modernize the civil service, concentrating on our vision for the 21st century and common principles, and looking at what changes to our approach to recruitment and development processes, interchange with other sectors, performance management, and valuing diversity are needed to support that vision.
>
> (HM Government Cabinet Office, 2002, www.cabinetoffice.gov.uk/moderngov/whatismg.htm)

Such an explicit commitment to diversity will be an important driver to any diversity change programme, certainly in the public sector. So establishing the need for the training is not just about the skills people need to be trained in: it is also about what is driving the need in the first place. The situation that gave rise to the need for a commitment to diversity may well hold many clues to what training might be required. These clues will in turn inform the needs analysis process. In other words, if you are asked to conduct a needs analysis for training in diversity, your point of departure should be whatever generated the request in the first place. Do not be satisfied with 'We've been told we need to do some training on this' or 'We have money left in the training budget which needs spending'. Check what is driving the request and who has made the business case for the training. Is the request for a needs analysis presupposing that training is necessary, or is a possible outcome a recommendation that some other intervention might be appropriate? All of these issues will help give you the bigger picture in which the diversity training is to be developed.

Of course some drivers are so significant that many of the above considerations become redundant. We have already mentioned *The Stephen Lawrence Inquiry* report as being a significant driver for police diversity training. The *Inquiry* made several recommendations about the need for police officers and civilian support staff to be trained in 'valuing cultural diversity'. So the actual need for training was a given – the only question to be answered was what the training would look like.

Terms of reference will also need to be established before you embark on a full-scale needs analysis. The sorts of thing that might usually be expected to be settled before you start are:

- The drivers for the training. (See the discussion above.)
- The budget available for the research, and whether a budget has been made available for the training.

- What access to the target population will be allowed/facilitated.
- Access to customers/receivers of the service provided.
- The human resources available to conduct the research.
- The expected outcome of the needs analysis. For example, it could be a report, a set of recommendations or a course proposal.
- Any constraints on what may be suggested. For example, a decision might already have been made as to how long the training will be. Whether any alternative delivery strategies are feasible, for example e-learning.
- The contact person who can speak for the sponsor.

Target population: knowledge/skills/issues

Once you have considered the bigger picture and background, and established terms of reference, the next step will be to focus on the target population. This will involve finding out a number of things:

- What diversities are represented in the target population? In other words, what individual requirements might need to be taken into account in designing the training? To neglect this aspect is to run the risk of introducing institutional discrimination or institutional racism into the very programme that is trying to address such problems. You might consider (see methodology below) that once you have identified the diverse groups in the organization, some of the needs analysis would be better done by engaging with specific groups in your research. For example, you might well find out more about the needs of part-time or flexible workers if you talked to them as a group, rather than in company with those who might well not understand their needs.
- What level are people at already? It may be important to find out at what level people feel themselves to be already in relation to diversity issues. If you were to find that a substantial number of people were already displaying many of the attitudes and values that support diversity, it would be necessary to research that deeper to find out why. Benchmarking across the organization might reveal this as well.
- What training have they already had? On the face of it this is an apparently simple question. Yet many organizations are quite poor at keeping efficient training records of staff, particularly in relation to training that does not lead to some sort of certification. Another problem that this might reveal is that even if individuals claim they had training some time ago, what does this say about what they know, understand or can do now? What will you be able to find out about the aims and objectives of such training? Was there any assessment of learning? We are not suggesting

these questions to make the thing sound more complicated than it really is, but if you are to do the job properly it is likely that you will have to answer them.

- Can the target population be grouped by relevant criteria that will make the design more focused? An example of this might be the roles that people perform. There might be people who have frequent contact with customers or those who receive the service. Their needs may well not be the same as those who work mainly internally. It may be the case that managers will have training needs that are different to those whom they manage. We used the word 'relevant' in relation to criteria quite deliberately. This is to avoid the suggestion that people can be grouped (for the purpose of training design) by any criteria that would merely tend to reinforce stereotypes or group people unfairly. Another point to consider is whether managers and staff should be trained together or separately. We have found in diversity training that there are advantages and disadvantages to both. On the one hand, people learning together as a community signals the fact that diversity is for all and there are no special cases. On the other hand, very often in diversity training managers come in for some criticism of the way they manage the diverse needs of people who work for them. So there is a decision to be made.
- What 'cultures' in the organization might get in the way? In other words, when you come actually to collect data, what might get in the way of your getting to the real issues? As we will see, a key source of the data you seek will be individuals and groups. If there is a culture of cynicism, for example, how will this affect your research? Will people be sufficiently open and honest if, for example, they are invited to a focus group to discuss the issues?

Benchmarking: where the organization is now

The practice of benchmarking is prevalent amongst many competitive organizations, and may have different focal points. One definition of benchmarking is:

> the continuous search for relevant best practices that lead to superior performance and customer satisfaction, by measuring against and learning from other parts of the company, competitors or companies recognized as leaders.

(http://www.benchmarking.btinternet.co.uk/)

Another much simpler definition would be:

> Improving ourselves by learning from others.

> (http://www.benchmarking.gov.uk/about_bench/whatisit.asp)

Benchmarking, particularly in the context of diversity, is a fruitful activity in needs analysis for a number of reasons:

- It helps us to learn about and draw on good practice. Different public and private sector organizations in this country are at very different points in terms of valuing diversity. If we know how we are doing in relation to others, the need for training or lack of it will be brought more into focus.
- It provides a means of control. By this we mean that benchmarking is a way of controlling some of the many variables in what we know about our own performance. In public sector service terms this is very important. So, for example, in a diversity programme an initial variable will be the way in which a diverse population views the quality of service it is receiving from a given service provider. A benchmarking exercise might try to capture those views, perhaps in different geographical locations where different authorities are providing similar services. Where do the differences in quality lie? How different is the perception of the public in different areas? Such information will help greatly in determining the training need.
- It supports evaluation. Where a benchmarking exercise has engaged with the satisfaction of the people receiving a given service, then it will be much easier subsequently to evaluate any diversity training programme that has been undergone to change and improve performance.
- It supports quality assurance processes. Benchmarking as a process may be used to develop new techniques for improving quality of service and efficiency. This in turn may have a role in informing the specification of a training need. For example, a benchmarking exercise might find that customer or staff satisfaction could be improved by the simple expedient of spelling people's names correctly. A focus on this could easily be built into any diversity training programme that was undergone. A check on the way names were being spelt could then be built into any subsequent quality assurance process.

Methodology: how it is to be done

So how do we gather all the information that has been discussed above? It is our view that data collection in relation to diversity is not the same as collecting data about something more tangible. There are many sources of data that may need to be tapped in order to get a rich picture of what the need is and therefore how to design the training. Figure 5.3 presents some of these sources.

Figure 5.3 *Sources of needs analysis data*

The target population relates to the people who will receive the training. In the section above we noted some of the things you will need to find out about the people who will be trained. To collect data from and about the target population you have a number of options:

* Training records – if they exist.
* Personnel files, which if examined with the appropriate safeguards, may reveal patterns in terms of annual and interim reports.
* Talking to people individually or in groups. Where you engage with individuals you will need to decide if the conversation is to be structured, unstructured or semi-structured. The advantage of the structured approach is that all such interviews will be consistent in terms of what is asked. The problem may well be that there is insufficient freedom for people to talk about the issues that are of concern to them. Semi-structured or even unstructured interviews might reveal more insights into what training is needed.

The drivers for the training, the possible existence of relevant occupational standards and the organizational need can be grouped together, as they will usually involve literature-based research, although they might possibly include ad hoc meetings with relevant stakeholders. Examples of such sources would be:

- minutes of meetings;
- corporate plans;
- business plans;
- policy documents;
- reports;
- results of inspections.

You will no doubt think of many more that are relevant to your own context.

Customers and people who receive the service represent the hardest group to get reliable data from, and yet in many ways they are the most important. Your choice of data collection method will be to a large extent determined by the budget you have for the work. Focus groups are time consuming and fairly expensive, but can prove to be a rich source of information. Beware that not all you hear in a focus group may be authentic. They do have a reputation for encouraging people to 'go with the flow' of the conversation rather than expressing their personal view. Having said that, we find their use to be preferable to the main alternative: questionnaires. Consider for a moment how much agonizing goes on over the development of a question for a referendum. Asking a question that will unambiguously mean what you intend it to mean to the respondent is notoriously difficult. Asking questions about diversity compounds the difficulty. At least in focus groups or interviews you have the opportunity to seek clarification.

USING STANDARDS

If you are routinely used to engaging with the specification of training needs, you may have been surprised or even frustrated as you read the section on training needs analysis. Why did we not refer to well-used phrases like 'skills deficit', 'training gap', 'performance need' and so on? The identification of such training needs is made considerably easier if specific standards of competence exist for the occupational area in question. While a trawl through the many sector organizations for appropriate standards will usually yield rich results, there are not many to be found in the area of diversity (but see the example shown as Figure 5.4).

In determining training needs you will find that for many occupational sectors there are well-defined standards against which to measure performance. National Training Organizations – reorganized and re-designated in April 2002 as Sector Skills Councils – have the responsibility for developing and promoting National Occupational Standards in a given area. Such standards play a vital role in the three general areas of:

- quality assurance;
- human resource management;
- human resource development.

To focus for a moment on human resource development, there are a number of specific functions that standards might have and these include the definition of training needs. Standards for human resource development can be used:

- to develop objective and clear selection criteria and to inform the recruitment process;
- to accurately assess learning and development needs, for both skills and the knowledge needed to underpin these skills;
- to construct learning and development plans to meet these needs;
- to check the content of existing learning programmes to ensure that they are comprehensive and reflect best practice;
- to develop new learning and development programmes and opportunities based on identified needs;
- to set objectives for learning and development programmes and opportunities so that their impact on practice can be measured and evaluated;
- to construct person specifications and job/role descriptions so that the expectations of individual performance are explicit.

A specific role of standards, then, is the accurate assessment of skills and knowledge needed for an individual to be competent in a given area. In Figure 5.4 we give an example of part of a unit of a suite of occupational standards that has been developed by the police service in response to the recommendations made by *The Stephen Lawrence Inquiry*. In this case the standards relate to competence in making sure there is proper communication with communities. It should be noted that we use the words 'occupational standards' without capital letters advisedly. For standards to be National Occupational Standards (note the use of capital letters) they need to be approved by the Qualifications and Curriculum Authority (QCA) for a

Sector Skills Council (formerly National Training Organization). The example in Figure 5.4, although occupational standards to which the police service is now working, has not yet gone through the process of validation by the QCA.

Consider for a moment whether the competence requirements set out in Figure 5.4 would be of use in defining your own training need.

Unit A1

Enable members of all communities to voice their issues and concerns

Element A1.3

Promote understanding of the role of the service and the rights and responsibilities of the public

Performance criteria

You will need to —

> a   make use of all formal and informal opportunities to explain the *role of the police* and the *rights* and *responsibilities of the public.*
> b   provide accurate and up-to-date information about policing plans and community initiatives for preventing and reducing crime and anti-social behaviour.
> c   make all written information available in language and formats that will be readily understandable by members of all communities.
> d   organize interpreting services when this will aid understanding.
> e   answer all questions accurately, seeking advice from colleagues if you are not sure about details.

Range

> 1   *Role of the police:* crime prevention; crime reduction; crime detection and investigation.
> 2   *Rights of the public*: to an anti-racist and anti-discriminatory police service; to an effective complaints procedure.
> 3   *Responsibilities of the public*: crime prevention; assisting the police in crime detection and investigation.
> 4   *Language:* plain English, main community languages.

Figure 5.4   *Example of occupational standards relating to diversity*

Underpinning knowledge
Conceptual framework

- why it is important to increase trust and confidence in policing amongst minority groups
- local policies, strategies and procedures about community and race relations
- the Victims' Charter; underlying principles and application to effective policing
- working knowledge of the underlying principles and relevant sections of the Sex Discrimination Act 1975/86, Race Relations Act 1976, Disability Discrimination Act 1995, Human Rights Act 1998, Disability Rights Commission Act 1999, Immigration and Asylum Act 1999 and Race Relations (Amendment) Act 2001 and how they should be applied within the individual's role and level of responsibility
- ethnic monitoring of data, police practice and community relations (Home Office circular 3/96)

Diversity and discrimination

- the positive benefits of diversity
- the beliefs, practices and traditions of the main cultures and religions; the cultural, religious and ethnic make up of the local area
- the reasons why individuals seek asylum; issues particular to asylum seekers

Communities

- key statutory and voluntary agencies, community groups and associations within area of work, including inter-agency and multi-agency partnerships
- effective channels and methods of communication with members of all communities
- types of opportunities available for promoting the service within communities
- methods of consulting with communities about their issues and concerns
- crime patterns in communities: contributing factors, levels and types
- the complaints procedure for members of the public

Cross-cultural communication

- barriers to cross-cultural communication and how to overcome them
- how to organize and provide translation and interpreting service

Figure 5.4   *(Continued)*

DESIGNING FOR AWARENESS

In Chapter 3 we mentioned 'awareness' in relation to learning to learn about diversity. In designing diversity training too there is an important issue around what is meant by 'awareness', since very often the claim made for this type of training is that the intention is to raise people's awareness of something. The issues for learning to learn were that we need to know what 'awareness' is commonly taken to mean, and more importantly, if someone's awareness of something is raised, in what sense can he or she be said to have learnt something? If 'awareness' is assumed to be a lower-level objective than the person being able to do something, or think about something, then in what sense can awareness have anything to do with training at all? In terms of design, it is important to be clear what awareness means, especially if this is framed as an aim or learning intention for the training.

A simple dictionary definition of awareness is 'a state of being aware; consciousness, especially a vague or indistinct form'. This implies that if you are aware of something, you might not be able to be specific about it, but might just be 'aware' of it. For example, you might be aware of someone's presence in a room without actually focusing on the person at all. This raises the question that when we speak of race awareness or diversity awareness, do we really mean that we want people to come to some vague or indistinct notion of it, or are we seeking something more profound? Most people engaging in designing diversity training would not be satisfied with outcomes that were so vague and indistinct. We believe that there is something deeper about awareness that we can engage with, that is helpful not only to the diversity training designer, but also to understanding what we are trying to achieve when delivering the training.

Marton and Booth in their book *Learning and Awareness* (1997) expound a much deeper view of what awareness is and how it relates to learning. Essentially their view of awareness is grounded in the experience of the world that we all have. If we take diversity as a phenomenon, we can say that different people will experience it in different ways. Now although as individuals we all by definition experience things differently, in reality for any given phenomenon there will actually only be a limited number of ways in which people experience it that are qualitatively different. We will always experience things in a context, and as the context varies so will our experience. So we come to Marton and Booth's view of awareness: that it represents the totality of the ways in which we experience something. You should see by now that this is completely different from the general use of the word. What does all this mean for the designer of diversity training?

• It means that when we are conducting a needs analysis there has to be clarity about what is meant by awareness, if that is one of the aims. If the sponsor of such training is under the impression that awareness raising is merely a low-level thing, then he or she might have unrealistic expectations of what can be achieved.

- It means that when we are designing the training it will be important to make sure that the training interventions include exercises to engage with the different ways in which learners might be experiencing diversity.
- Finally, it means that we should not be satisfied with a less powerful definition of awareness. This would leave the way open for people to engage in the training in a way that does not adequately challenge their experience in terms of attitudes, values, beliefs and prejudices, all of which are inextricably linked with the way that diversity is experienced.

AIMS, GOALS AND LEARNING INTENTIONS

All of the above leads us to the next phase of the design, namely being specific about what learning outcomes you are expecting. So far we have not mentioned anything about objectives, and you will have noticed from the heading of this section that we have not used the word and prefer 'learning intentions' instead. We fully concede that being specific about what the training is intended to do is an important feature of the design. In fact there are a number of good reasons why we need to do this.

- Those who sponsor and manage such training have a right to be told what the training is intended to do. They usually either hold the budget or in some way are accountable for it.
- Learners not only have the right to be informed about what the training is about, they will learn better if they have a 'route map' of where the training is leading.
- Designers need to have specified what the intentions are before settling on the design. This will not only ensure that the programme is designed to be comprehensive, but also that the specification of the learning intentions will usually suggest suitable methods of delivery and possible ways of assessing whether any learning has taken place.

The two reasons why we are uncomfortable with defining the training in terms of objectives are, first, that we do not believe the term has yet thrown off its association with behaviourist approaches to training. We discussed in an earlier chapter the argument that in many ways diversity is a matter for education rather than training. The way needs to be left open for learners to explore, with the trainer as their guide and facilitator. They need to explore their own attitudes, values and beliefs. They need to explore the issues. Such activities are not easy to capture in the rigid way that behaviourist objectives are meant to be written.

Second, pure objectives have too much focus on the trainer. They echo an approach that is teacher centred and where the measure of success is more about whether the trainer achieved the objectives rather than whether the learner actually learnt anything.

So we prefer the term 'learning intentions' because it emphasizes learning and because it expresses an intention that leaves the way open for other outcomes. Within learning intentions we are less concerned with the use of classic objectives verbs such as 'list', 'specify' 'explain', and more comfortable with 'explore', 'consider' and 'reflect on'.

We include the term 'goals' because in organizing the learning, a layer in-between the aim and learning intentions is often useful. It is not uncommon to see a number of aims for a particular programme of training. In our view this has the potential to cloud the issue. A good clear statement of aim should sit on its own and act as a guiding light for where the training is going. Refer to Figure 5.5 to see the sort of hierarchy we have in mind. The goals will act as useful statements to help organize the work, and the learning intentions will cover specific content material.

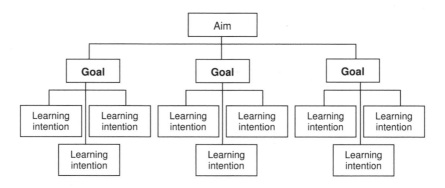

Figure 5.5   *Aim, goals and learning intentions as a hierarchy*

Let us now put a practical slant on all this and look at a hypothetical example. We have in mind a two-day training course for senior managers. The organization they lead is on paper committed to diversity, and it is intended that in the fullness of time all of the staff will undergo some sort of training in diversity, although it has not yet been planned. For the time being the senior team members have allocated two days to work on their own issues. After a great deal of needs analysis (see above) it has been agreed that the senior management team need most to work on:

- their own attitudes and values;
- the meaning and manifestation of institutional racism and discrimination;
- how best to promote diversity in the organization.

They all consider themselves to be leaders, so something around leadership needs to be included.

The aim, goals and learning intentions for such training might look like those we have suggested in Figure 5.6. They are not complete, but just intended to give a flavour of what we mean. In passing it might be worth reflecting on the extent to which even what we have shown could realistically be achieved in a two-day session.

IMPLEMENTING A DIVERSITY PROGRAMME

Once you have done all the needs analysis, carefully considered the aims, goals and learning intentions for the training, and made them explicit, it is time to design the actual training programme. As we have already mentioned, other chapters contain discussion and possibilities for delivery and evaluation, so we do not intend to go into that level of detail here. Having said that, there are a number of issues about implementing a diversity training programme that we have learnt from experience and feel are worth sharing. They represent a fairly eclectic set of hints and tips that have not been dealt with in detail elsewhere in the book. They are presented in no particular order.

Consider the skills of the trainers

While we would argue that diversity training is a speciality and requires special skills, the reality is that all too often mainstream trainers are thrown in at the deep end to deliver this sort of training. We say elsewhere that this is both dangerous and unfair. But if you know that the trainers for whom you are designing a programme do not have much experience in the field or lack the necessary skills, you will need to take that into account in your design. As a minimum in these circumstances we would suggest that the trainers who will have the responsibility to deliver should get at least some preparatory training themselves in the intended programme.

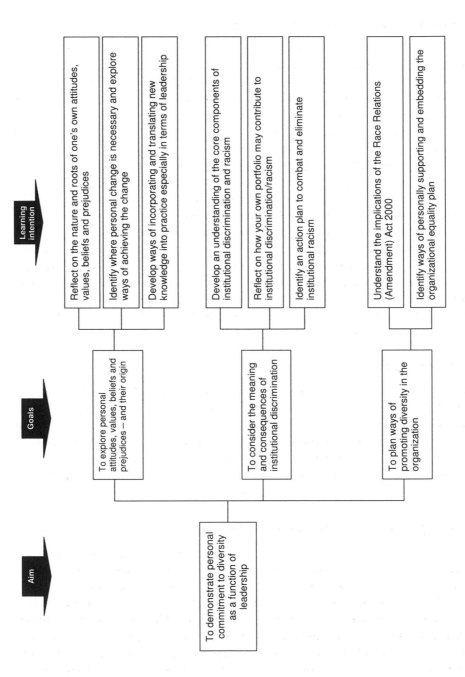

Figure 5.6 *Example of an aim, goals and learning intentions session*

Consider the needs of the learners

Some of us are used to speaking in public, speaking in groups, or even role playing. Where training is intended for the whole organization, there will inevitably be people who are not used to such things. They may feel very nervous and reluctant to speak. Imagine how you might feel if one of your first experiences of group learning was to share your attitudes and values with a group of strangers. While we exaggerate to make the point, when designing programmes you do need to take such factors into account. Think about using non-threatening ice-breakers, warm-up exercises or early working in pairs as ways of alleviating nerves and helping people to learn better.

While we are making points about the needs of learners, remember that if you are using contributors from the community, their needs are equally important. Good practice suggests that consideration should be given to holding the event either in a neutral location or at a venue located in the community. It is all too easy to forget that having to come to a formal location can be an intimidating experience in itself. Also consider what people will wear. If formal suits and ties are normally appropriate for your participants, will this have the effect of marginalizing members of communities who come to join in and support your training?

Consider fallback positions

The best-laid plans for training can go wrong, and it is often worth considering what you will do if this happens. For example, if your whole training strategy depends on the use of theatre, what will you do if one or more of the actors cannot attend? Some theatre companies may be able to provide an understudy, but this will not always be the case. One solution might be to video your scenarios early on in the programme so that you will have something in reserve should it be needed.

Making plenary sessions more effective

Typical training sessions that you design will include some group work which is then followed by everybody coming back for a plenary session of feedback and discussion. Very often this will involve the groups reporting back on their discussions or presenting the results of the exercise on flipcharts. It is not unusual for groups merely to read out their flipcharts without much comment. The more groups that have to feed back, the greater the potential for the process to become boring and repetitive. Even worse, if this takes place in a large room people may not be able to hear properly or see the flipchart. You could consider allowing a short break before the feedback to allow key points to be presented in a computer program such as Microsoft PowerPoint. Alternatively groups can be asked to write their key points on acetate for display on a larger screen with an overhead projector. Other ideas for more stimulating ways of dealing with plenary feedback include discussion panels made up of representatives from each group, and the facilitator interviewing group members to find out what they have learnt.

Briefing and debriefing community participants and learners

An important feature that needs to be built into the design if community contributors are to be used is briefing and debriefing. This should also include the participants. All involved need to be clear about the purpose of community involvement. The issues discussed may well be highly emotive, for example if people are talking about their experience of racism or discrimination. Clear guidelines need to be established before the event about respect, valuing each other and most of all listening and not responding by merely being defensive. After the event participants and contributors should be debriefed to ensure they have the opportunity to talk through the experience and offload any anxieties that may have developed.

Refreshments

We have mentioned before that diversity is not so much something we study as something we aim to live. Trainers, for example, need to 'walk the talk'. It goes without saying that any training event that focuses on diversity should itself model good practice. So it is worth remembering that plans for refreshments and meals should reflect a concern to be inclusive rather than exclusive. Not everybody drinks tea or coffee. Some will not take caffeine for religious reasons, so have water or other soft drinks available. Does the lunch menu take account of Halal meat and vegetarians? Can you safely assume that all the food will be labelled? Thoughtlessness in this area can end up as a good example of institutional racism.

Build in a feedback mechanism

It is very common in diversity training for participants to raise issues within the organization that really need to be dealt with in some way by someone outside the group. For example, if a group is discussing unfairness towards members of the organization, many specific issues might be raised: arrangements for people with a disability, or a culture of acceptability of homophobic humour, or perceptions of unfairness in selection for promotion. It is helpful to negotiate with the group to log these on an 'issues sheet' and secure agreement to feed them back to a relevant person who is in a position to do something about them. An organization that is serious about diversity should also make arrangements to update people on what action has been taken.

KEY LEARNING POINTS

In this chapter we have invited you to consider approaches to designing diversity training.

- We noted that a systematic approach to training would involve in its simplest form an investigation of the need, design, delivery and evaluation.
- Needs analysis will involve engaging with the drivers and terms of reference, understanding the target population, benchmarking internally and externally, and an understanding of appropriate methodology.
- We introduced the possibility of using standards where these exist as a good way of identifying relevant competencies.
- Awareness was discussed as something that needs to be defined clearly, particularly where 'awareness' is the aim of the training.
- We noted that a useful way of specifying the training and leading into the design phase is to define a clear aim which is then supported by goals and learning intentions.
- We ended with a number of hints and tips around implementing a diversity training programme. These included the skills of trainers, the needs of learners, having fallback positions, the importance of briefing and debriefing, and making sure that the training is inclusive of all and has a mechanism for providing feedback to the organization.

Chapter 6

Diversity Training: Challenges and Issues

By the time you have worked through this chapter we hope that you will have:

- thought about the issue of confidentiality and taking risks in diversity training;
- considered the relationship between institutional racism and institutional discrimination, and how these impact on organizations and training programmes;
- been able to take a perspective on diversity that is implied by the 'journey analogy';
- explored the implications for individuals and groups for changing the way they see the world;
- considered the issues around what authority trainers have to engage with other people's attitudes and values;
- identified the factors that contribute to stress in trainers and those engaged in organizational change.

INTRODUCTION

At the beginning of the book we suggested that diversity in many ways represents a special case in terms of training and its management in organizations. This is largely due to both the wide variety of diversity that there is in most organizations, and the impact that diversity can have on so many aspects of organizational and individual behaviour.

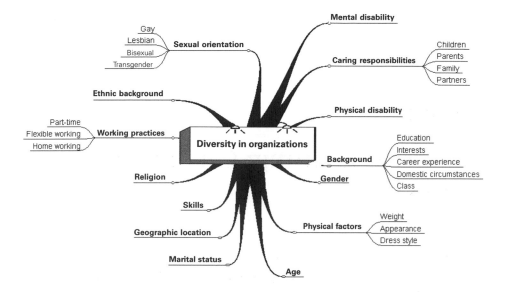

Figure 6.1 *Diversity in organizations*

In Figure 6.1 we have tried to capture something of the range of diversity that will be found in most organizations.

It is our view that the effective handling and management of some of these issues is critical to the success of a diversity change programme. In the next few sections we will explore some of these issues in more depth.

CONFIDENTIALITY AND TAKING RISKS

Talking with trainers about the issue of confidentiality is guaranteed to produce pained expressions which reflect the difficulties that the issue of confidentiality can raise. Try the little exercise in Figure 6.2 below which invites you to explore why confidentiality might be a challenge that needs to be met.

We suspect that you will not have ticked anything in the 'never' box and that most of your ticks will be in the 'sometimes' and 'always' columns. What can we make of this? There are a number of issues that are raised in relation to confidentiality and taking risks. In summary these are issues around the relationship between confidentiality and risk, and the process of diversity training.

	Always	Sometimes	Never
1. People say things in diversity training that they regret			
2. People get angry in diversity training			
3. Individuals feel hurt by what gets said in diversity training			
4. People express anger in diversity training			
5. People 'clam-up' in diversity training			
6. Individuals try to stay in a 'comfort zone' where they believe they cannot be challenged			
7. People say that what they believe is a personal issue and not the business of anyone else			
8. People believe that saying what they feel may be risky			
9. People are unused to expressing feelings in peer groups			
10. People believe that promises not to breach confidentiality are worthless			

Figure 6.2   *The challenge of confidentiality: tick the answer that in your experience most applies*

The relationship between confidentiality and risk

Let us begin with a couple of stark statements:

People will only effectively learn about diversity if they are prepared to take risks in their learning.

They will only take risks if they feel safe to do so.

In Chapter 3 we explored the implications of learning to learn about diversity. A crucial aspect of this was the notion of 'self-awareness'. As a learner I need to work through my own attitudes, values, beliefs and prejudices. This includes not only what they are, but from where they originate. In other words, what experience has led me to adopt the position I do? In order to get in touch with my attitudes, values and so on, I am likely to have to take risks in training. This is because at some stage I will need to say something about my position to the group. This can be a risky thing to do, because others in the group may not agree with me, or even worse may take a stance that exposes my prejudice and negative feelings towards other groups. There may even be members of diverse groups undergoing the same training, and what I think, feel or believe may be offensive to them. As we saw in the interactive exercise in Figure 6.2, this may lead to anger, 'clamming up' or other responses that will be difficult to manage. So exposing attitudes is a risky thing for the trainer, the group and the individuals in the group. Yet it is our firm belief that it is a crucial component of effective training and education in diversity. People need to be challenged but they need to feel safe to be challenged. This is where there is a close relationship to confidentiality. One thing that is guaranteed to make me feel unsafe about saying what makes me tick is if I feel that others will take that outside the group and gossip about what I have said. So I need to have some reassurance that what I say will be said in confidence.

The process of diversity training

To achieve a level of confidentiality where participants feel safe to risk disclosing very personal attitudes, values, beliefs and prejudices is the aspirational goal of most diversity training. The sad fact is that the aspiration has to be set against the real world reality that most people believe that confidentiality cannot be achieved. Although you can control to whom you report the content of a training session, you have absolutely no control over who those other people might tell. So if, as a trainer, you make a confidentiality contract with participants in a group, you have no meaningful way of making sure that the contract is respected outside the training room.

So we have a dichotomy. We need people to take risks to learn. They will take risks if they feel safe to do so. They will only feel safe to do so if a number of components are in place.

We would recommend that the management of all groups seeking to learn diversity includes some form of 'ground rules' as part of the process. Figure 6.3 shows ground rules that we have used in the past and which seem to work in favour of creating the safe climate that we seek.

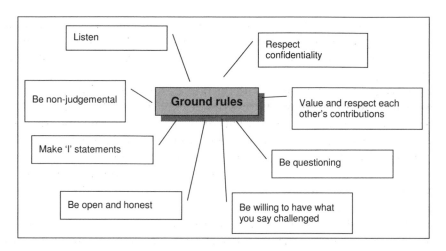

Figure 6.3   *Example ground rules*

You might like to consider each ground rule in turn and make a judgement about how useful you think it would be in creating an appropriate climate for learning. It is useful to have a brief discussion with the group about what is being agreed to in each ground rule. For example, making 'I' statements is particularly useful for helping people to take ownership of their position. Otherwise it is very easy for people to speak as if they are representing the views of others when in fact they are expressing what they as individuals believe or think. It is also important to discuss what they mean by 'respecting confidences'. From your point of view, you can make an absolute assurance (if you are in a position to do so) that participants are not under assessment and that no report about what an individual has said will be made. If, because you are conducting the training for a client, you do need to report back some of the content of the training, you need to be open and honest about that. What you can of course do is reassure participants that nothing will be attributed to an individual.

Before we leave this section one further issue needs to be confronted: what do you do if someone makes an overtly racist statement? Does confidentiality extend that far? We suggest a number of possible tactics:

- Agree with the group at the outset that you would like to reserve the right to speak to individuals privately should this prove necessary. In this way you can talk to people outside the group and discuss with them the implications and consequences of a position they might hold.

- Always challenge inappropriate comments at the time they are made and adjust the process as necessary to deal with them. In some organizations, you as trainer may actually be liable for not dealing with racist behaviour in a group.
- Encourage other members of the group to respond to inappropriate or discriminatory comments. How did they experience what was said? What does that say/illustrate about what we are trying to learn about diversity?
- Do not let participants get away with making their feelings known through non-verbal means without being challenged. This may be body posture, 'tutting', sniggering, or a whole range of other non-verbal expressions of dismissiveness or disagreement. Such expressions have the same power as if someone actually expresses the thought in words, and they need to be challenged. Be careful not to immediately challenge with your own interpretation of the behaviour. Check first. For example, 'John, I noticed you seemed to snigger when Ruwan said that. What did that mean?'

INSTITUTIONAL RACISM AND DISCRIMINATION

We have included a discussion of institutional racism and discrimination in this chapter on challenges and issues because, in our experience, on the one hand the phenomenon (certainly for organizations and institutions) strikes at the core of what diversity is all about, and on the other hand all diversity programmes themselves need to be examined for their potential to perpetuate it. So in this section, our exploration will include:

- a brief analysis of the Macpherson (1999) definition of institutional racism;
- the difference between institutional racism and institutional discrimination;
- strategic and tactical approaches for ensuring that diversity change programmes do not in themselves perpetuate institutional racism or discrimination.

The definition

February 1999 saw the publication of the Macpherson Report of the inquiry into the death of Stephen Lawrence, a young black man who in 1993 had been the victim of a racist murder. The police were shown to have failed in a number of ways, not least in failing to gain a successful prosecution of five white men who were, and remain, strong suspects for the crime. The inquiry concluded that the poor, even inept, performance of the police could be blamed in part on 'institutional racism', which was defined in the Report as:

> The collective failure of an organization to provide an appropriate and professional service to people because of their colour, culture or ethnic origin. It can be seen or detected in processes, attitudes and behaviour which amount to discrimination through unwitting prejudice, ignorance, thoughtlessness and racist stereotyping which disadvantage minority ethnic people.
>
> (Macpherson, 1999: 28, para 6.34)

The challenge of institutional racism is to achieve a proper understanding of how it relates to your own organization or institution. Think about the definition for a moment. What do you consider to be the key words or phrases? How do they relate to the institutions or organizations in which you are involved? It seems to us that some of the keys to unlock the meaning of the definition are:

- collective failure;
- appropriate and professional service;
- colour, culture or ethnic origin;
- processes, attitudes and behaviour;
- unwitting prejudice, ignorance and thoughtlessness;
- racist stereotyping;
- disadvantage ethnic minority people.

Collective failure distinguishes institutional racism from individual racism. McKenzie (2000) notes that it was Carmichael and Hamilton (1967) who first coined the term 'institutional racism' with the intention of distinguishing it from individual racism, the former having an overwhelming importance over the latter. Where institutions collectively fail to provide an appropriate and professional service they tend to have racism embedded in their rules, policies and procedures. That is not to say that any of these effects represents overt racist intentions. The effect, however, is that where policies, procedures and so on have been developed by white majorities (usually white men), then other groups – in the case of this definition, ethnic minority groups – are disadvantaged by their exclusion from the development of the policies. Attitudes and behaviour are those held by the majority in an organization. Such attitudes are usually characterized by making assumptions that exclude others. This is turn may lead to unwitting prejudice, thoughtlessness and racist stereotyping, the effect of which will be to disadvantage ethnic minority people.

The definition was originally aimed at the police service in this country, but it quickly became apparent that very few institutions are immune from the possibility of institutional racism.

Institutional discrimination

The same principles that drive institutional racism equally apply to other forms of institutional discrimination. Diversity recognizes differences between different groups and acknowledges the fact that to be treated fairly, people need to be treated according to their needs. A number of individuals are at risk of being the victims of discrimination because of the assumptions and thoughtlessness of which organizations and institutions are capable. Refer back to Figure 6.1, which illustrates some of the diversities that may be recognized in most institutions in this country. You will hopefully make the connection that all of these groups might in some way be the victims of institutional discrimination. A key feature of effective diversity change programmes is to make certain that they eliminate any potential to institutionally discriminate.

Strategy and tactics for eliminating institutional discrimination

The overall strategy for any institution in terms of meeting the challenge of diversity must include an intention to eliminate the reality of, and any potential for, institutional racism and discrimination. Given the scale of the problem of racism, its widespread negative effect and the pernicious motivation that often underlies it, we would argue that 'race' should not be lost in the overall strategy on discrimination. So while it is true to say that all discrimination against diverse groups needs tackling, racial discrimination should not be marginalized or subsumed as an issue. In Chapter 2 we saw that the Race Relations (Amendment) Act 2000 places a statutory duty on key institutions to promote good race relations. For this reason, institutions will ignore race issues at their peril.

Tactics for eliminating institutional racism

So what can we do to help make certain that institutional racism and discrimination are eliminated? Try answering the questions in Figure 6.4. You might

My institution: *Tick the box which, in your expereince, reflects how your institution is doing*	Fully meets	Partially meets	Does not meet
Has a process for regular reviews of policies and procedures			
Retains staff because they want to work for it			
Knows what diversities are represented in it			
Projects an image which is inclusive, not exclusive			
Has an absence of internal cultures which exclude certain groups			
Is representative of society's ethnic composition			
Is a place where people feel safe to be who they are			
Keeps good records that enable it to rapidly identify where things might be going wrong			
Regularly and genuinely consults with the people to whom it provides its service on all aspects of its policy			
Is driven by its values			
Provides training in diversity for its staff			
Recognizes that the people in it have differing needs			
Respects religious needs			
Has leaders who promote and role-model a positive orientation towards diversity			
Has an effective method for people to air their grievances in a safe way			
Provides a way for people to talk about how they are feeling in the organization			
Listens to its people			
Invests in meeting diverse needs			
Researches the diverse needs of its stakeholders			

Figure 6.4   *Eliminating institutional discrimination and racism*

like to take a number of different perspectives in answering the questions, for example as a business manager, a personnel officer, or as a trainer.

We suspect that some of the questions may have been difficult to answer. We also suspect that you did not rate many of your answers as 'meets'. For most institutions there is much work to be done to make certain that institutional discrimination in all its forms is eradicated. How will you contribute to that process?

THE JOURNEY ANALOGY

Research by Clements (2000) indicates that many trainers see diversity training in terms of an analogy of taking the students on a journey. We have included it here as an issue because it is a useful way of thinking about diversity training and education, and reflects some of what is needed for the attitude change that diversity training seeks to achieve.

Trainers often talk about the 'journey' as an object in itself. In other words, metaphorically taking the students on a journey is seen as a legitimate excursion, even if there is some uncertainty about the final destination. In Chapter 5 we discussed approaches to the design of diversity programmes. The journey analogy is important in this context because very often organizations legitimately want clear statements about the objectives of a diversity training programme. From the trainer's perspective, however, although the objectives for a given session may be explicit, there can be little certainty about where an individual's journey in training might begin and end.

The trainers in the research also made some quite clear statements about the nature of the training that the journey implies. For example, there is a very strong learner orientation and an assumption that this (the journey) is something the learner will need to do for him or herself. The trainer will take on the role of guide. Phrases such as 'you make links for yourself', 'personal discovery', 'personal exploration', 'got a grasp of who you are', 'to understand themselves', 'matter of the heart', are all used in the context of being on a journey in the training. One trainer summed it up as:

> I look at it very much like a journey, a journey of self-discovery but because it is internal to this organization then it is, yes, good, that's a journey about self-discovery and I'm glad you've made that because the important thing is that you make connections, you make links for yourself so if you internalize it we have now gone into the attitudes and behaviour stuff. . . . If you have got that and are taking the people

through the journey then out of that comes hopefully, this internalized . . . is their own way of dealing with people and therefore it con-
firms their professional behaviour.

The journey therefore needs to be one of self-discovery: connections and
links need to be made for oneself. In other words this is not something that
the trainer can do for the learner, and it will include internalizing about
attitudes and behaviour. It could be argued that the starting point for a
learner's journey is knowledge of his or her own position in relation to the
issues. The journey may not be an easy one, in that self-discovery may be an
uncomfortable process for both trainer and learner.

Drawing on both what the trainers said and our own experience, we can
summarize this issue as:

* The analogy of the journey is one frequently used by trainers to describe
  one of the objects of diversity training.
* The analogy implies the need for the training to be learner centred.
* This training will revolve around self-discovery for the learners.
* Learners need to be encouraged to make links between what they find
  and their professional life.
* A major aspect of the self-discovery will be the acceptance of personal
  prejudice, developing an understanding of the source of this and making
  links with the person's professional life.
* Being on a journey with the trainer may have the effect of making the
  training less threatening, and will help to engage the learner's interest.
* It is to be expected that the process will be an uncomfortable one, but this
  in itself will be an indicator of quality diversity training.
* A successful outcome of the journey is where the student has been
  empowered to make his or her own choices.
* The journey should be made in the context of the individual's life experience. The training in itself may represent a point in the person's life
  where he or she thinks about his or her stance on issues in a way that he
  or she may not have been challenged to do so before.

Pause for reflection

Reflect on your own journey in diversity. What was your starting point?
What were the key milestones? Try to describe what it would be like if
you felt you had 'arrived'.

CHANGING THE WAY WE SEE THE WORLD

In Chapter 3 we took a mainly theoretical view of how people learn to learn about diversity. A critical component of this is recognition that a diversity change programme will inevitably involve people in changing the way they see the world. This may be limited to where an individual comes to recognize that there is room for many and diverse ways of seeing the world. Or it may be that an individual actually changes the way he or she sees things. In this section we want to think through some of the practical implications of all this.

As a point of departure, take a look at the statements in Figure 6.5.

I treat others as I like to be treated
I treat others as they deserve to be treated
I treat all people the same
I treat people according to their needs
I treat others as they want to be treated
I treat others according to the way they treat me

Figure 6.5   *Tick the statement(s) that most closely match what you believe*

How easy was it for you to do this exercise? If you were to do a similar exercise in a group, the strong probability is that different people would tick different options. Why is this? It is in part due to the fact that people have different understandings of and attach different meanings to the statements. For example, on the face of it, 'I treat others as they want to be treated' means that I am intent on meeting people half-way. It could also mean, however, that I am the one who decides the way in which people like to be treated. This gives a completely different slant. The reality is that our differing responses are largely based on the way we as individuals see the world, and that view is anchored in our values, attitudes, beliefs and prejudices.

A challenge in diversity training is to bring others to see, and be able to see, the world differently. In the words of a trainer, being able to 'consider issues from a different angle', and this seeing something differently may well involve an adjustment to one's way of seeing the world. How can we engage with this challenge?

- Ensure that variation is built into the learning experience (see Chapter 3).
- Recognize that coming to see things in a different way may or may not be a sudden experience for the learner.
- Accept that a process of exploration will precede it.
- Make sure that this exploration has an internal and external focus. It may be knowledge of issues but it must also include knowledge of self. In practical terms this means that any process for diversity training should include engaging with and exposing people's attitudes and values.
- Design exercises that will ensure that all individuals in a group have the opportunity to address their own issues.
- Constantly expose and challenge assumptions.
- Recognize and take account of the fact that coming to see the world differently and having our assumptions challenged is very likely to be an uncomfortable, even painful, process, and that appropriate support and safety need to be factored in to diversity training.

AUTHORITY TO ENGAGE WITH ATTITUDES AND VALUES

A major issue that confronts diversity trainers is the extent to which they feel they can engage with attitudes, values, beliefs and prejudices, or the extent to which a learner may allow this to happen. This is both an issue and a challenge, since not all trainers believe that they have the authority to engage with attitudes and not all learners agree to allow it to happen. On a recent diversity course the session opened with a short exercise to give the participants the opportunity to express their objectives for the day and any concerns they had about the training. One participant openly expressed his view that he was there under duress, he regarded the whole diversity pro-gramme as unjustified thought control, and that his only objective was to get through the day without 'blowing his top'. For good measure he added that he did not believe in diversity. Now in terms of process, such behaviour is not too difficult for a facilitator to deal with. But it can only be dealt with effectively if the facilitator is sure of his or her ground and both has and believes that he or she has authority to engage with such people.

Most organizations engage in diversity training programmes because they are publicly committed to diversity. Such organizations are likely to have a diversity policy, a diversity strategy, a mission or vision statement, a statement of corporate values or whatever. The bottom line is that members of an organization – especially when they are being paid by it – can reasonably be expected to sign up to its corporate values and mission. All people, of course, have the right to think and believe what they like, but to adopt a closed attitude – and in the case of the example above a very narrow and blinkered view of the world – effectively means that such a person is untrainable.

The importance of the issue is again reflected in the research conducted by Clements (2000): a majority of trainers interviewed talked about the authority (or lack of authority) that they felt they had to engage with learners. This was particularly in relation to raising their awareness of attitudes, values, beliefs and prejudices.

Pause for reflection

How would you deal with a situation where a learner said, 'I challenge your right to take me through this process, I do not want to go into discomfort, I do not want to address my way of seeing the world, I'm fine with the one I've got'?

Compare your thinking with this trainer who expressed certainty about his authority:

> Well, partly in terms of defending that would be to say, 'Well, you know you are not here as a free uninhibited human being. You are here as a member of an organization which has specific aims and purposes and the bottom line is that you are paid wages to work within certain parameters.'

Not all trainers seem so certain about the source of their authority. For example:

A: I don't think we have got the right to change people's values and attitudes. I think we have a responsibility to make people consider their own values and attitudes and what effect they can have on other people.

Q: What right do you have to try and change someone's world-view?

A: Right? No right at all.

Another trainer expressed it in terms of ethics and morals:

A: I think it is an ongoing feature because I think there is an ethical and moral issue anyway and the extent to which you can meddle with people's hearts and minds . . .

We can summarize the issues concerning the authority that trainers have to engage with attitudes and values:

- Trainers need to know that they are mandated by the organization to challenge learners and take them into areas where the learner may feel uncomfortable.
- Learners need to know that the trainers have that mandate. A very frequent way of this happening is for a very senior person in the hierarchy to 'open' the course – with a personal statement of his or her own and an emphasis on the organization's commitment to the diversity training.
- The extent to which a trainer may attempt to change a person's way of seeing something may be an ethical or moral issue. Having said that, as we have said elsewhere in the book, the bottom line is always the law as expressed in the various conventions on human rights. If a learner needs a trainer to engage with his or her attitudes and values in order to help the learner have a higher regard for the rights of others, then so be it.

COPING WITH TRAINER STRESS

Some interesting research was conducted some years ago which had the intriguing title *Equal Opportunities Can Damage Your Health!* (Kandola *et al*, 1991). It was found that people engaged in equal opportunities who worked in organizations had higher than average mental health problems. It is our experience that the situation is not much better today. In fact, reports of trainers engaged in diversity training feeling they are being harassed, or worse bullied, are not uncommon.

We have made the point several times that when people are challenged about their attitudes, values, beliefs and prejudices the emotional temperature can rise dramatically. The process may well be painful for the individual; it will be equally stressful on the trainer. Very often trainers will be delivering their training in the context of a diversity change programme in an organization. Individuals coming to training sessions may well be attending because they have to rather than because they want to. So right from the start there is likely to be conflict. Other individuals, although attending willingly, are likely to believe that the problems of diversity are not of their making, and they are therefore not open to be challenged about their own attitudes and so on. Where trainers are delivering to such groups day in and day out, the effects on them can range from demotivation and a feeling of being demoralized right through to trainer 'burn-out'. Signs and symptoms of stress are all

Table 6.1   *Signs and symptoms of stress*

Physical	Emotional	Mental
Heart pounding	Moody	Forgetfulness
Headaches	Irritable	Loss of concentration
Sweaty palms	Depressed	Poor judgement
Indigestion	Anxious	Disorganized
Shortness of breath	No sense of humour	Confused
Cold hands	Hostile	Loss of interest in
Sleeplessness	Nervous	things
Too much sleep		Numeric errors
Fatigue		Negative self-talk
Nausea		Bad dreams
Diarrhoea		
Tight stomach		
Tight muscles		

too common. Consider the physical, emotional and mental manifestations of stress shown in Table 6.1. Have you, or has someone you know, experienced any of these, either on their own or in combination?

A common cause of trainer stress is a feeling that a group is in some way bullying the trainer. What do we mean by bullying? It is generally accepted to be: offensive, intimidating, malicious or insulting behaviour, an abuse or misuse of power through means intended to undermine, humiliate, denigrate or injure the recipient. Our experience has always been that learning groups have the capability to exercise considerable power over a facilitator. Even a minority of people in a group, if they are vocal enough, can actively try to undermine or humiliate a trainer. Very often, if the trainer is not sure about the authority for the training, or feels unskilled to deal with aspects of it, then the result will be a trainer who suffers the stress of bullying.

We need to conclude this on a positive note, so let us consider for a moment what can be done about the problem. There are a number of things that a trainer can do for him- or herself, as well as a number of things that the organization in which the training is taking place can do to provide support: see Figure 6.6.

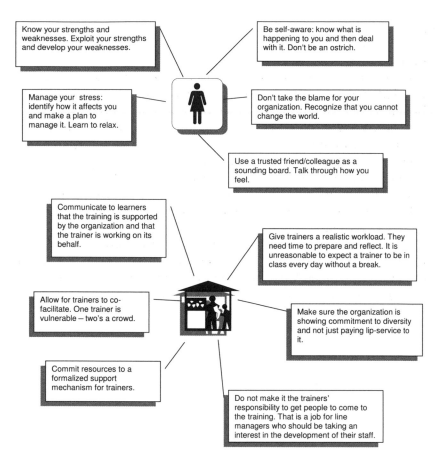

Figure 6.6   *Trainer stress: what individuals and organizations can do*

KEY LEARNING POINTS

In this chapter we have explored some of the issues and challenges in a diversity change programme. Specifically we have:

- Considered the importance of confidentiality to learning, the relationship of confidentiality with taking risks, and the need to create a 'safe' learning environment.
- Looked at institutional racism and institutional discrimination in terms of how they are defined and how they manifest themselves in an

organization. We hope you carefully considered a number of questions that amount to tactics for eliminating both institutional racism and discrimination.

- Examined the way trainers talk of diversity training as a 'journey'. You were challenged to reflect on your own journey into diversity.
- Thought about what it means to see the world in a certain way. In doing so we noted that people can often hold very different world-views and a key element in embracing diversity is to develop an acceptance of the value of these different ways of seeing.
- Noted that not all trainers and diversity managers feel equally empowered to deal with the issues of diversity. Organizations need to show demonstrable commitment to diversity and its business benefits, and not just pay lip-service to them.
- Considered the way in which trainers often suffer stress and burn-out if they do not manage themselves properly and are not properly supported by their management. We concluded with some ideas about what trainers and organizations can do to combat the problem.

Chapter 7

Tactics for Teaching and Learning Diversity

By the time you have worked through this chapter we hope that you will have:

- considered the advantages and disadvantages of a range of tactics for teaching and learning diversity;
- identified some of the advantages of small-group work in diversity training;
- explored a range of facilitative techniques that are useful when working with groups.

INTRODUCTION

We have tried to make the case elsewhere in the book that teaching and learning diversity are often quite different from teaching and learning other subjects. One of the key reasons for this is that diversity training can be very destabilizing for people. This is often because people have their sometimes 'cosy' view of the world challenged in a way that they normally would not. Such challenges can be a very uncomfortable experience, and some would say an essential ingredient of changing attitudes and sometimes values. A trainer we know regularly conducts community and race relations training and regards his sessions as unsuccessful if, in their post-course evaluation ('happy') sheets, members of the course say they enjoyed themselves. Of course some people do enjoy being challenged, but our experience is that, by and large, getting to grips with change can be a very uncomfortable experience. So if you are involved in training, then you should be prepared for a difficult time.

In the section that follows we outline a number of classroom-based activities that you might like to consider using in a diversity training programme. For each we have described the activity, suggested some advantages and disadvantages, and then offered an analysis of the activity. It is important, of course, as with any training, that you have considered the likely implications of any given activity. The question that overarches all others in this regard is 'How will it help people to learn?'

ROLE PLAY

Role play is now universally used in all sorts of training context. An essential ingredient of role play is that real-life scenarios are engaged in and individual role players behave as they would in those situations. The two broad types of role play available to trainers are planned, where the scenarios are worked out in advance either by the trainer or the course participants, and spontaneous. The latter usually arises where a discussion point has been made and the trainer or the participant immediately takes on a role and the issues are explored there and then.

Advantages

- Role play is an extremely good method of engaging with people's lived experience and enabling role players to find out how they react to different situations.
- It is cost effective and requires few if any additional resources.
- Spontaneous role play can be quick and effective at exploring individual learning points.

Disadvantages

- Some people, particularly if they are not used to it, find role playing quite threatening. We have often run groups where it is quite difficult to encourage participants to take part and get the most from it.
- Truly effective role play relies heavily on the way the session is fed back. There is little point in a really well worked out scenario if the follow-up discussion does not engage with the issues that were raised.
- Planned role play may have to depend on considerable preparatory work. In working with various organizations we have found that the most effective role play engages with actual examples that are grounded in the

culture of that organization. People will recognize the situations as ones they may have experienced. All this requires a great deal of preparation on the trainer's part.

Analysis

Role play can be a very powerful method of exploring many of the issues raised by diversity. As with most methods used in this type of training and education, it provides a way in to the issues and will invariably open up rich discussion. We said in Chapter 3 that part of the model for 'good' diversity training has the object of raising awareness in individuals, both of things inside of themselves – self-awareness – and of things external to them. Role play is particularly good for the former. It can provide an opportunity for individuals to learn about their own prejudices, assumptions, and way of seeing the world. Helping learners to make sense of what they have experienced in a role-play situation is vital. A good grounding for this type of feedback is to spend some time with the participants in agreeing what actually took place, what was said, and how each participant viewed it from his or her own perspective. Time invested in this will pay dividends because one thing that will inevitably happen is that you will open up variation for the learner. The participants and those observing will by definition have different perspectives on what happened, what was said and how the players felt about all this. This will effectively lead in to discussion to bring out key learning points, but the whole process will need to be led and managed by the trainer and requires considerable skill.

PSYCHODRAMA

Although we have not used this method of group work, we have included it as an option because of its close relationship with role play. Psychodrama is a methodology based on the work of Jacob L Moreno (1889–1974), a Romanian psychotherapist who worked in the United States from 1925. The method is best described by way of the stages that a typical (classical) psychodrama exercise goes through. Martin Gill (www.dryw.freeserve.co.ukClassicalindex.html) describes these stages as:

- Warm up: a period where group cohesion is encouraged and individual spontaneity stimulated.

- Identification of a protagonist: a person (or persons) in the group chooses to work on a particular instance in his or her life experience.
- Agreeing a contract: this stage defines what the person will work on, why he or she wants to do so, and a clarification of the issue for the individual. For example, 'I want to work on why I react negatively to gay and lesbian people in my workplace.'
- Scene setting: an area is set aside in which the protagonist will work. Everybody needs to be able to see and hear clearly and the 'audience' may be involved to help create the right atmosphere and mood.
- Action phase: 'insight' is achieved for the protagonist through actions which are orchestrated by the psychodramatist. As with other 'insights' that learners achieve in training, the insights they may accrue in psychodrama may be either sudden – where the person experiences the 'penny dropping' – or gradual, developing after a period of reflection.
- Enactment: the protagonist is encouraged to display his or her inner and outer experiences. He or she may also take the opportunity to explore 'as if' situations, where the person visualizes how a situation could be different for him or her.
- Closure: a closure scene will usually be related to what the protagonist has been acting out. Often the psychodramatist will direct this, and the aim will be to build concrete suggestions for the future.
- Sharing with the group: in this stage the opportunity to de-role is taken and people in the group share their experience of what has happened. Sharing represents a re-entry into the here and now.

Advantages

- Psychodrama can be an effective method of getting in touch with an individual's lived experience and making sense of it.
- Some people come to diversity training with a range of emotions such as guilt, anger, confusion and resistance. Psychodrama can be useful to deal with these emotions in a way that is helpful for the individual's growth.

Disadvantages

- Psychodrama is very time consuming and must be worked through properly if individuals are not to be left at best emotionally in limbo, and at worst emotionally damaged.
- Leading psychodrama is a process that is beyond the usual skill level of a trainer who has not had specialist training in it. Because of its power there is the potential to cause more damage than good.

- The focus on the individual may not be suitable for working in a training programme where the groups are large.

Analysis

Psychodrama has its roots in, and still has strong connections to, psychotherapy. The British Psychodrama Association is involved in training psychodramatists and works to a strict ethical code. We suggest that although the method may be useful, you make a serious assessment of your own skill level before purporting to use psychodrama as a method in your own training. If you are interested in exploring this further, however, two useful web links are:

www.metta.org.uk
www.psychodrama.org.uk

THEATRE

Many diversity training and education programmes involve the use of theatre as a way of exploring and opening up the issues. Typically professional actors are used to act out scenarios that are based on the real-life experience of the organization. This is followed by individual or group work to work through the issues, then the learning points are discussed. An interesting recent development in the use of theatre is to use actors to play out lines written by participants and directed by them. For example, a scenario might involve three characters each taking a different perspective. A pre-prepared scenario is started, and then at a certain point the drama stops and participant groups tell the characters what to say next and direct the action. In this way groups can explore the effect of certain words or behaviours but at the same time stay detached from them.

Advantages

- Professional actors are best able to re-create scenarios based in the culture of an organization. This can be made even more powerful if care is taken to make sure the language is correct. For example, in our experience different organizations have many different names for annual reporting, and often these are referred to by abbreviations. Annual performance appraisal (APA), performance development review (PDR), performance action plans (PAP) and so on are all examples of different names for basically the same thing. Where the scripts have been carefully prepared to use the right terms they can have more impact.

- A second key advantage (but see below under disadvantages because this can be turned on its head) is that individual participants do not need to role play. We noted above that some people find role play threatening, and our experience is that many participants are relieved to find that actors will be doing the role play for them.
- Well-briefed actors can be used to engage in conversation with the participants. For example, after a scenario has been acted out the learners might have the opportunity to find out more about a particular situation before working on a problem.
- Where the training is part of a programme in which the whole organization is to be trained, using actors can help to achieve consistency and corporacy of message, since all the learners will be examining the same issues.

Disadvantages

- Using actors has a monetary cost associated, and you will need to make the business case for using extra resources when budgets for training are set.
- Unless you are using an acting agency which will guarantee to provide understudies, there will be a problem if your whole training strategy for a given day hinges on the actors turning up. A replacement fallback position is not always easy to devise.
- From a teaching and learning standpoint there is disagreement about whether it is more effective for learners to watch someone else doing something or to engage in it themselves. In role play and psychodrama, individuals have an opportunity to work through their own experience. Watching actors working is one step further removed from engaging with this experience.
- Actors need to be booked well in advance, and if you are conducting a whole programme of training you will lose some flexibility in setting dates for your courses.

Analysis

Our experience is that the advantages of using professional actors outweigh the disadvantages. This is particularly so in working in contexts where the participants have not routinely been exposed to role play as a training method. Very often with diversity training, particularly if the object is 'awareness', the course may be of one day's duration only. This means that you do not have time to develop sufficient confidence in participants to engage in role play, and using actors can easily overcome this. From the learners' perspective it is important that with most scenarios they are briefed to take notes as necessary, as there is little time to develop characters or plot. Some theatre companies will develop the scripts for you if they are given access to your training needs research material (see Chapter 5, Designing diversity training).

VIDEO

Phil Race (2001: 22) cites a conference he attended where a constant theme was, 'Video is one of the most highly developed training media yet invented but remains one of the least well used.' There can be little doubt that using video can be a very effective method of opening up issues. Another possible use of the medium, if your budget will not stretch to the regular use of actors, is to shoot your own video of the 'trigger' scenarios and then use that instead of live actors. A number of companies specialize in the type of video that will stimulate your learners to learn about issues of diversity.

Advantages

Video can:

- be an excellent method for opening up discussion;
- allow for consistency of message as it can be used many times over with different groups;
- be paced to the needs of the learner as well as the demands of the training session (given that attention spans are usually very short, how much video is shown at a time can be tailor-made to the need);
- be a relatively inexpensive learning resource.

Disadvantages

- Video can go out of date very quickly, even though the underlying message may not have changed. Learners will be used to high-quality bang up-to-date documentaries on television, and most training video material will find it hard to compete with such quality.

- You will need equipment for showing the video. You will have to arrange for it to be available and working, and to know how to use the equipment properly.
- A good deal of preparation is needed to make certain that the right clips are shown at the appropriate time.

Analysis

Video is a powerful tool in the toolkit of the diversity trainer, but it does need to be used effectively if learning is to be maximized. To draw on Phil Race's article (Race, 2001) once again, some useful points about using video can be made:

- Choose video for what it can do best. In diversity training terms this means the ability to convey emotion, feeling, body language and so on.
- Remember that concentration spans are usually measured in minutes.
- If you have data projection facilities, then short video clips can be embedded into a presentation program such as PowerPoint. This makes them very easy to access.
- Involve the learners in what they should be looking for, or what perspective they should be taking as they watch the video.

Two websites that we have come across might prove useful leads for the types of video that are particularly suitable for diversity training:

www.mhie.ac.uk
www.videoarts.com

DISCUSSION

It may seem an obvious thing to say, but diversity training will rely very heavily on discussion. The success of this should not be a hit or miss affair, but is very often under the direct influence of the trainer/facilitator. Let us first consider some of the advantages and disadvantages of discussion, then think about some more issues relating to the use of discussion in diversity training.

Advantages

- Learners need the opportunity to discuss issues with each other, or with people who bring a particular minority perspective, in order to learn effectively.
- Discussion enables the facilitator to move the group into areas that will address the learning intentions.
- If one of the learning intentions of the training is to bring attitudes, values, beliefs and prejudices to the surface, it is inevitable that learners will need to vocalize these. Discussion will provide a forum for this.

Disadvantages

Most of the disadvantages of discussion arise from its being badly managed, rather than the method in itself.

- One problem for the trainer who facilitates a discussion is always how to involve all members of the group. If an individual says very little, there is no real way of knowing whether he or she is fully engaging with the learning.
- Large groups can be intimidating for people and may well cause a great reluctance to speak in a discussion.
- Discussion, particularly when participants are really engaging with the issues, can be very difficult to manage in terms of time. You as facilitator will be reluctant to stop a group that is discussing well, but this will need to be balanced against the process for the session.

Analysis

Discussion is probably the most important tactic to employ in diversity training, but it needs to be managed well. Facilitators need to be skilled in managing groups and have a high level of awareness of what is going on. It can be very exhausting, because as facilitator you need to keep one pace ahead of what is going on, you need to be monitoring the non-verbal communication to pick up messages, and you need to keep monitoring and encouraging progress. All this requires skill. As facilitator you will also need to make conscious choices about your role. For example, at times it will be appropriate to be directive; at other times you will need to negotiate with the group and work in partnership; at others still the best thing for learning will be to allow the group autonomous freedom. All this will need a facilitator who has a high level of awareness of what is going on in the group at any particular time. Discussion will be most fruitful and inclusive of all participants, even the reluctant ones, if you are able to engender a climate of safety, where people feel confident to say how they are feeling as well as what they are thinking. The trick is to do all this at the same time as challenging people to get below the surface of what they would normally talk about.

QUIZZES

A frequently used way of opening up discussion is to use a quiz of some sort to allow participants to test their knowledge of diversity issues. Typically the group feedback of the answers will be the opportunity to open up discussion.

Advantages

- There is an almost unlimited range of information suitable to use in a quiz.
- People seem to like quizzes. Consider the popularity of quiz programmes on television and radio, and pub quiz nights.
- Quizzes can be a fun and non-threatening activity for learners, and may go some way to creating a climate of safety, provided they are not dressed up as a test of some sort and individuals do not feel humiliated if they do not know the answers.

Disadvantages

- Quizzes can easily be trivial and facile if they are not constructed properly.
- Questions about 'factual' things like the ethnic minority make-up of the country may do little to help people engage with learning the real issues.
- Undemanding quizzes may have the effect of patronizing learners or, perhaps worse, giving them the false impression that the quiz represents all there is to the subject.

Analysis

Our view is that while quizzes have a role to play, it is important to avoid the disadvantages they represent if they are to contribute effectively to learning. If you do design a quiz as a way into discussion, try to make sure that it addresses the learning intentions for the session and presents a challenge to the group. Questions that have answers that may be a surprise for the learner, and tend to open up deeper issues such as racist assumptions, may be most useful. An example of this might be, 'Which country currently accepts most refugees?' (The answer does not lie in Europe!).

THE VALUE OF SMALL GROUP WORK

One of the ways to overcome the disadvantages of some people's reluctance to engage in large groups is of course to divide participants up into smaller units. How this is done will depend on the circumstances: for example, it may be appropriate to randomly select members of smaller groups. If you have a sense of who is quiet and who tends to speak a lot, you may be able to construct groups that take account of this. A small group made up of people who seem reluctant to engage may encourage them to open up, while a small group of people who have a lot to say may work well. It is often a good idea, if there are several opportunities to engage in small group work, to make sure that people have an opportunity to work with different participants as the session progresses. There are several advantages to this which include maximizing the sharing of life experiences and world-views, giving participants an opportunity to work with others who may be more or less dominant, and quite simply making the whole process more dynamic and interesting for the learners.

One of the issues that small group work raises for you as facilitator is that you will temporarily lose touch with what is going on in some groups. This is magnified if the groups are working in different rooms. The practical difficulties that this may raise include:

- You will not know (at least immediately) whether the group is actually focusing on the issue in hand. It is not uncommon to find that a small group has lost touch with the original brief and has started discussing something that, although it may be interesting and important for them, does not address the issue you were hoping to deal with.
- If your instructions to groups about an exercise have not been explicit, the groups may not produce the expected output.
- Small groups working on their own are not always good at keeping to time. Some, for example, may engage with a task in a shallow way and finish quickly. Others may really get to grips with detail and take much longer.

The solution is, of course, to make sure that people do understand what is expected of them and are quite clear what output is expected. If you want them to write things on flipchart paper for later use, people usually need to be reminded to use large letters! You might also consider appointing someone in the group to be a timekeeper to help keep the group on track. If it is intended to ask someone to speak on behalf of the group in a plenary session, it is sometimes wise to nominate the person before the exercise begins. Alternatively, if you are working by giving more autonomy to learners, get the group to elect someone to speak on its behalf.

ISSUES FOR FACILITATORS

Facilitation is a whole subject in itself. There are a number of models of facilitation which are beyond the scope of this book. Having said that, diversity training does raise some issues for facilitators which need to be mentioned. These issues tend to be around specific behaviours that may manifest themselves in diversity training.

Resistance

It is very common for diversity facilitators to report resistance by participants. We have said elsewhere that diversity issues can often cause people to express resistance to being open to the issues. Such resistance is a significant factor in diversity trainers feeling stress or even being bullied. Some manifestations of resistance that we have come across are:

- Refusal to take part in activities, exercises or role play.
- Deliberate attempts to change the agenda to issues with which the participant feels more comfortable.
- Refusal to switch mobile phones off.
- Feigning a need to go to a meeting during a training session.
- A concentration on issues rather than feelings.
- Staying silent, but – unlike a shy person – leaking resentful non-verbal communication.
- Statements calculated to undermine the process, the facilitator or the subject.

Dealing with resistance is one of the most challenging things a facilitator has to do. This is partly because it takes skill to deal with and partly because those who show resistance are often those who most need to be open to the issues if they are to learn and change. A number of facilitative tactics can be employed to engage with resistance. They all assume that the facilitator has both the confidence and the skill to challenge it:

- Listen and watch for overt or subtle signs of resistance and address them at the time. It does not help you or the individual to leave it until later.
- Make the consequences of resistance clear to the group. It may be useful to refer back to any ground rules that have been set. For example, a consequence of resistance may be that a person breaches a ground rule of valuing and respecting others in the group, or of being open and honest. Another fairly self-evident consequence of resistance is that it will inevitably get in the way of the individual's and others' learning.
- Ask the others in the group how they feel about what is going on. What effect is it having on the way they are feeling about the process?
- Be strong as a facilitator in keeping the process on track. Deflect attempts to bring discussion to a level which trivializes the subject or does not engage with how people feel.
- Remember and hold on to the fact that if people are being resistant, then you are probably succeeding in the task. If all participants are 'happy' with the training, there is a possibility that you have not challenged enough.

Anger

Anger is another common feature of diversity training, and again a challenging emotion to cope with. There cannot be many of us who actually enjoy anger as an emotion, especially in the context of training. This is not when people engage robustly in argument, it is when people get 'hot under the collar' about an issue and may shout, go red, shake, or even go in for anger-expressing gestures. If a group member gets angry it can be problematic because it will very likely make you, or others in the group, feel very uncomfortable or even anxious.

- Be professional. You are there to facilitate learning and that must stay the aim. Recognize that a person getting angry may well be experiencing a severe challenge to dearly held assumptions or prejudices. Anger may be the only way individuals have of dealing with uncomfortable truths they are finding out about themselves.
- Stay calm. Hold on to your confidence and keep cool. You can deal with it.

- Do not take it personally. Anger is often displaced on to a facilitator who is seen to represent the organization. However much it might feel like it, it is very unlikely that it is directed at you as a person, unless of course you are responding in kind.
- Do not rise to the bait. It is all too easy to meet anger by becoming angry yourself, and probably saying things you will later regret. Try also to be aware of your non-verbal reaction to the situation. You may be saying calming things while at the same time non-verbally leaking what is going on inside. You can safely assume that people will notice this.
- If necessary, take time out and call for a break to allow things to cool down. You could use this time to speak to an individual privately and try to get to the bottom of why he or she is reacting in such a way.
- Be prepared for anger by working out in advance how you respond to anger. We all cope with it in different ways, and some are more affected by it than others. Forewarned is forearmed in this case, and knowing how an angry outburst might affect you will help enormously by your being ready for it.

Silence

When people are silent in a group it is usually because they are shy and lack confidence or they are being silent as a means of offering resistance. When whole groups are silent, it can have the effect of making the facilitator feel quite vulnerable, and in some respects the process may have faltered. The causes of whole group silence are many and various, and in our experience include:

- Asking the wrong question, at the wrong time. For example, a question that asks about feelings or seeks disclosure of an attitude or prejudice will rarely work well if the group has not yet formed an identity and reached a stage of feeling safe to disclose.
- A closed question to which the answer is so simple that people suspect a trap and no one offers an answer because people believe they will look silly. The group may be looking for a more complex response that was never your intention.
- A group using silence to try to manipulate the facilitator. With the best will in the world we will sometimes upset one or more people in a group. Often this can be through leakage of your own frustration with the group if, for example, you think they are not making enough progress, or avoiding the issues. Groups may either consciously or unconsciously

collude to make their feelings known to the facilitator, and silence will be used to signal this.

Some practical tactics that can be employed to deal with silence include:

- Try to distinguish between reflective silence and silence that is prompted by some other reason. It may be that in fact you have asked a very good, deep question that has made people sit up and think. For example if you were to ask, 'What support do you need in your work?', how reasonable would it be to expect a snappy reply? In reality people will need time to let that percolate, then they will need to reflect. It may well be that they have never thought about it. So do not be afraid to allow plenty of time for this reflection, and do not allow yourself as facilitator to be intimidated by the fact that no one is responding immediately.
- Be aware of the effect your own behaviour may be having on the group. If you are working mainly by doing all the talking, the group may well adopt the expectation that you are there to 'feed it' and will stay silent accordingly. So check yourself; are you saying more than you need? Have you said or done anything that may have caused the group to clam up? Are you providing the right stimulus to get people talking, sharing and disclosing?

KEY LEARNING POINTS

- In this chapter we have considered a range of tactics that may be used in diversity training. There are of course many others that you will be familiar with and may wish to try out. The key learning point in relation to these tactics is, as with all training, that failing to plan is the equivalent of planning to fail. We have tried to show that there will be both advantages and disadvantages to whatever method you choose to employ. As a professional you will need to balance these against each other and decide what is most appropriate, not only for your target population but also for your own skill level. The test should always be, how will it enable people to learn?
- We noted a number of advantages of small group work in diversity training. Not least among these is the way in which small groups enable people to share their lived experience and also to engage with the experience of others. This is a vital component of good diversity training.

- The chapter concluded with a summary of some difficult behaviours that facilitators may encounter in diversity training and how to deal with them. A key thing to bear in mind, especially for those who organize such training and commission the trainers, is that diversity training, unlike most other types, requires a high level of facilitator skill and self-confidence. Organizations have a duty to ensure that the people they use to do this work are appropriately skilled.

Chapter 8

Evaluating and Assessing Diversity Training

LEARNING INTENTIONS

By the time you have worked through this chapter we hope that you will have:

- assessed the extent to which you currently undertake any evaluation of diversity training;
- considered a number of definitions of evaluation, and thought through their purpose;
- examined five major approaches to evaluation and assessed the relative strengths and weaknesses of each approach;
- considered different models of evaluation and how they could be applied to the evaluation of diversity training;
- thought about the relative benefits and disbenefits of each model, and appropriate means of assessing diversity training.

INTRODUCTION

This chapter is intended to provide you with an introduction to evaluation. As with other chapters in this book, we have drawn heavily on research and theoretical models. However, we have tried to demystify what can be quite turgid reading, and have attempted to look at the practical implications of evaluating training.

The chapter begins with an attempt to answer what to some are seen as two questions that are immediately filed in the 'too difficult' section: Why is there a need to evaluate training? and How do I evaluate training?

Evaluation is much discussed and often neglected. It is often placed in the 'too difficult tray' or seen as an unnecessary and expensive overhead. Our view is very different. We recognize that training is an expensive commodity, not only in terms of the event itself but also in respect of organizational and individual commitment. In Chapter 2 we highlighted the business case for diversity training, but without evaluation how can you determine whether or not you have achieved the required business benefits? Of equal importance is the need to retain the organizational knowledge pool. Without evaluation how will an organization retain its corporate knowledge, how will it learn from emerging good practice, and how can it benchmark performance against other organizations? If the training has been established in order to raise awareness and knowledge of new legislation, how can you judge whether or not the training has met the identified need? We recognize that evaluation is not easy, and it certainly does not come without cost. However, we are firmly of the belief that evaluation of training is an important feature of any diversity programme.

Exactly how do we evaluate training, and can we really identify the costs and benefits of training? One of the first issues to determine is who will undertake the evaluation. You have a number of options, including developing an in-house expertise, using consultants from commercial training or evaluation organizations, and employing academics. While it is beyond the remit of this chapter to identify the specific strengths and weaknesses of each approach, you should take some time to consider exactly what approach to evaluation is best suited to your organization and its training requirements. For example, we worked with one organization that had employed consultants with a very specific approach to training, development and evaluation that was completely at odds with the culture and expectations of the organization. The result was a very expensive national programme of training which met with enormous resistance from practitioners and was the subject of another expensive fundamental review and redesign some three years later.

This chapter attempts to demystify the subject of evaluation so that you are better able to select an appropriate evaluation methodology.

EVALUATION

Before we proceed any further let us try a little health check. Tick the boxes in Figure 8.1 which most accurately describe your approach to evaluation.

To what extent do you currently:				
	Never	Sometimes	Often	Always
Assess whether or not the training event has met the learning needs of the learners?				
Assess whether or not the training has improved the knowledge or skills of the learners?				
Assess whether or not the training event has improved the workplace performance of the learners?				
Assess whether or not the training has improved the organization's performance?				
Assess whether or not the training has led to identifiable financial benefits?				

Figure 8.1   *Evaluation health check*

We will come back to this figure later in the chapter, but before we do so let us have a look at how evaluation has developed as a tool for inclusion in the management of diversity toolbox.

The roots of evaluation

Evaluation is a tool which was developed in the 1950s as a means of assessing the impact of wide-scale government initiatives, programmes and policy (Easterby-Smith, 1994; Pawson and Tilley, 1997). It is therefore an academic discipline which has its roots in the social sciences; however, it is only recently that evaluation has been applied to training.

Definitions of evaluation of training

Although evaluation is relatively new as a concept, a number of researchers have tried to define it. Patten (1978) developed a fairly complicated definition in which he describes evaluation as involving the systematic collection of information about the activities, characteristics and outcomes of programmes, personnel and products for use by specific people to reduce uncertainties, improve effectiveness and make decisions with regard to what those programmes, personnel and products are doing and affecting.

Bramley, who tends to specialize in the evaluation of training, states that 'Evaluation of training is a process of gathering information with which to make decisions about training activities' (Bramley, 1996: 5).

Thorpe (1988) offers a more detailed definition of evaluation within the training context. He sees evaluation as 'The collection, analysis and interpretation of information about any aspect of a programme of education and training as part of a recognized process of judging its effectiveness, its efficiency and any other outcomes it may have.'

So if there are competing views as to what evaluation is, can we agree what we want evaluation to do? In other words, what is the purpose of evaluation?

The purpose of evaluation

Over time evaluators have developed different ideas as to what they see as the purpose of evaluation. Easterby-Smith (1994) identified four purposes of evaluation which have evolved since the 1950s.

Proving

The original purpose of evaluation was to prove whether or not the training event had led to any change in knowledge or skills. This would normally require some kind of pre- and post-training measurement, and was often seen as a kind of 'scientific experiment'.

Improving

In the 1970s some evaluators were not so concerned with the outcomes of the training, as with putting into place some kind of continual improvement process.

Learning

In the next decade some educationalists believed that evaluation should be an integral part of the overall learning and development process, and as such the training event was continually a subject of inspection and change.

Controlling

With public sector organizations becoming increasingly accountable and subject to performance measures, and the private sector concerned with profitability, the use of evaluation to control training is increasingly popular.

In our experience it is useful to determine the purpose of evaluating training for two reasons. First, deciding what you want the evaluation to do will help you to identify the most appropriate evaluation methodology. Second, particularly if you are employing an external third party to undertake your evaluation, you need to understand their methodological approach before agreeing their commission. It is often the case that evaluators will adopt their preferred approach, and you should ensure that both the methodology and the way in which the findings are presented will meet your organization's requirements. We will now look in more detail at the major schools of evaluation.

Schools of evaluation

As noted by Easterby-Smith (1994), there are five major schools of evaluation comprising:

- experimental research;
- illuminative research;
- the systems model;
- goal-free evaluation;
- interventionalist evaluation.

Experimental research

As we noted above, evaluation grew out of the social sciences in the 1950s, and the first evaluation studies used methodologies well established in this discipline. The basic idea here is to establish if there is any relationship between cause (the training) and effect (improved knowledge or skills), and to demonstrate that any changes in outcomes are attributable to the training event. Thus there is a tendency to use quantitative questionnaires and other comparative analysis tools, using control groups and pre- and post-training measurement.

Illuminative research

Illuminative research methodology was developed as a stark contrast to the scientific approach. The key features of this approach are as follows:

- Observation of the training event is followed by further enquiry and attempts to provide an explanation.
- There is a progressive focus on the key issues that have been identified as a result of the first stage, involving extended interviews with course participants.
- General principles are identified as a result of the second stage, and findings are placed within a much broader social context.

This approach includes a number of principles:

- While there is a fairly strong commitment to qualitative research methods, this does not discount the use of questionnaires or attitudinal measurement.
- The research should be conducted by a neutral outsider.
- It is argued that the main purpose of this approach is to enable the wider community to have much greater awareness of the programme.
- The evaluator should not be concerned with making specific recommendations to improve the training programme.

The systems model

While there are a number of variations on this theme, there are three main features of the systems-based approach:

- First there is a need to devise objectives for the programme.
- Second there is a requirement to identify the outcomes of the training event.
- Finally there is a desire to provide those involved in the delivery of training with feedback regarding the ability to match outcomes with objectives.

This approach is often seen as validation, and there is a need to distinguish internal validation from external validation. Internal validation is defined by the Department of Employment as 'a series of tests and assessments designed to ascertain whether a training programme has achieved the behavioural objectives specified'. External validation is described as:

A series of tests and assessments designed to ascertain whether the behavioural objectives of an internally valid training programme are

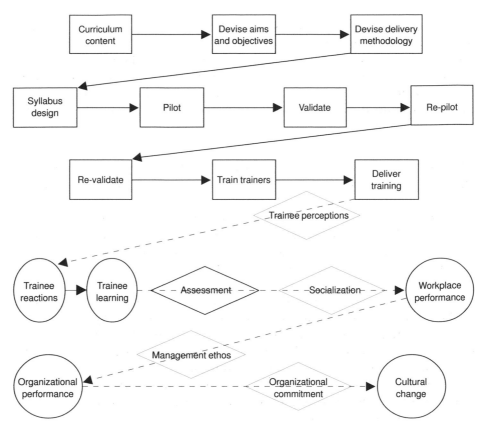

Figure 8.2   *Training delivery: inputs and outcomes (adapted from Easterby-Smith, 1994)*

realistically based on an accurate initial identification of training needs in relation to the criteria of effectiveness adopted by the organization.

This process is all inclusive and is said to be concerned with examining the totality of the training event, including an assessment of inputs, outcomes and costs.

In Figure 8.2 the solid lines describe the linkages between those events leading up to the training delivery, while the dotted lines lead to outcomes that might result from the training delivery. The difficulty in this approach is establishing beyond reasonable doubt that the trainee reaction and/or trainee learning and/or changes to workplace performance are the direct result of the new training event. Any identified change might be the result of some other extraneous event such as the individual's preferred learning style or any additional learning which takes place outside the learning event. These and other factors are represented in the diamond boxes.

The provision of feedback to trainers is an important element of this model, particularly where there is some element of central control over the training design.

Goal-free evaluation

This model was developed to contrast with the former model's reliance on objective setting. It advocates an approach in which the evaluator should take absolutely no notice of any specified aims and objectives. Supporters of this model contend that this is the only way an evaluator can determine the true value of the learning event, and that the evaluation will typically consist of lengthy interviews and observation of both the training event and workplace performance. A three-stage approach is advocated within this model:

- Extensive interviews should be conducted with all stakeholders, who should be asked to set out what they perceive to be the objectives of the programme. This will enable the evaluator to assess the 'true value'.
- The evaluator should not be concerned with examining whether or not the desired outcomes have been achieved. He or she should be more concerned with identifying any unanticipated outcomes.
- Evaluators should also concentrate on the processes of the training event rather than the outcomes.

Interventionalist evaluation

While there are a number of labels that have been applied to this approach, the two most commonly used terms are responsive evaluation and utilization focused evaluation. Both these approaches share similarities with the goal-free approach by being more concerned with the training activity rather than the results of the activity. They take into account the relative value placed on the learning activity by all stakeholders. However, responsive evaluation differs from goal-free evaluation in that it is not so concerned with distancing itself from the aims and objectives of the programme, and recognizes that there are occasions when other evaluation processes, including preordained methods, may better meet clients' needs.

Furthermore the responsive evaluation has been identified as containing a number of fundamental factors:

- The evaluation must start with identification of all stakeholders and a process of collating, debating and exchanging their relative concerns.
- There is taken to be no single version of absolute truth relating to the identified concerns.
- It is assumed that any suggestion of cause and effect cannot be identified from a single mechanistic process; it must be confirmed by a number of independent observers.
- It is taken that all stakeholders have an equal status and that their versions of truth have equal value.

A more pragmatic version of this approach was developed by Patton (1978), who recognized the respective influence of different stakeholders and that there would be contrasting needs. Patton also accepted that an evaluation can consist of a mix of quantitative and qualitative methods, although research reports should not rely on scientific jargon and should be written in plain language.

A clear difference between this approach and the illuminative method is that the former encourages the evaluation to identify the client's concerns and to directly address those concerns during the evaluation. The major feature of models within the interventionalist approach is that it encourages stakeholders to take action as a result of the evaluation data.

Having looked at the major schools of evaluation, try to identify the relative strengths and weaknesses of each approach.

How does your assessment compare with ours? (See Table 8.1.)

The five schools of evaluation have led some training specialists to devise models specifically designed to evaluate training.

EVALUATION MODELS

The three principal models are those devised and developed by Kirkpatrick (1976), Hamblin (1974) and Warr, Bird and Rackham (1970). However, a number of commercial organizations are having to justify the cost of training and development, and there is an increasing need for an evaluation model which is able to quantify the benefits of training in cost terms. After looking briefly at the three principal models we then examine how the benefits of training are being expressed in monetary units as a calculation of Return on Investment (ROI).

Approach	Strengths	Weaknesses
Experimental research		
Illuminative research		
The systems model		
Goal-free evaluation		
Interventionalist evaluation		

Figure 8.3 *Strengths and weaknesses of evaluative approaches*

Kirkpatrick's four-level model

Kirkpatrick's model consists of four levels as follows:

- **Level 1: Reaction.** This level of evaluation attempts to measure the trainee's reactions to the training event, including an assessment of the training methodology, the training content and whether or not individual training needs have been met.
- **Level 2: Learning.** This level is concerned with identifying whether or not the training event has increased the trainees' knowledge, skills or understanding.
- **Level 3: Behaviour.** Level 3 attempts to measure any changes to workplace behaviour or performance that have resulted from the training event.
- **Level 4: Results.** Level 4 is concerned with evaluating whether or not the training has led to organizational improvement.

While it is acknowledged that Kirkpatrick's model is the most widely used in current training evaluation practice, there are some detractors who see his model as simplistic and flawed.

Table 8.1   *Strengths and weaknesses of evaluative approaches*

Approach	Strengths	Weaknesses
Experimental research	• Use of questionnaires makes data collection and analysis relatively easy. • Clients and other stakeholders can influence questionnaire design. • Some stakeholders can be impressed by the 'scientific' approach.	• Sample sizes need to be extremely large if meaningful data are to be established. • Control groups generally need the same antecedents and characteristics as the experimental group and it can sometimes be assumed that control groups will not be affected by the absence of the new training under evaluation. • Measurement may be relatively simple in the case of single observable behaviours. In practice there can be a tendency to boil down multiple behaviours to form single observable behaviours. This is especially the case in the area of diversity training. • In many cases it is not certain that any observable changes in behaviour are the direct result of the new training, ie cause and effect are not sufficiently proven.
Illuminative research	• Initially the evaluator is seen as independent and neutral. • The evaluation is seen as comprehensive and	• There is a danger that evaluators are not seen as independent as they become immersed in the training event.

Table 8.1 *(Continued)*

Approach	Strengths	Weaknesses
	takes into account wider social influences.	• Some sponsors do not see the approach as having sufficient scientific validity or reliability. • The evaluation can take an excessive amount of time to complete.
The systems model	• It is systematic, which can appeal to non-evaluation specialists. • It can be relatively cost effective compared with other approaches. • It is well received by those who favour performance management processes.	• Critics of this approach are concerned that the reliance on predetermined objectives is too restrictive. • The emphasis on outcomes can be seen as overly mechanistic and while it might be applicable to measuring knowledge acquisition, it is not as easy to measure attitudinal change or changes in workplace performance. • The resulting data will generally assist with decisions on whether or not to continue with a particular training event. • This method is less successful when assisting with identifying how to improve the training event.
Goal-free evaluation	• It is very comprehensive. • It can reveal findings that would not have been identified by other approaches.	• This approach has been found to be particularly labour intensive and costly (it is mainly used in the evaluation of radical educational programmes,

Table 8.1   *(Continued)*

Approach	Strengths	Weaknesses
		particularly where extensive funding is available). • By its very nature (and name) it is seen as unsystematic.
Interventionalist evaluation	• The approach is likely to be seen as relevant and more likely to meet the needs of clients and other stakeholders. • It is likely to be more flexible than 'pure scientific' models. • Reports are more accessible and more easily understood than those which rely on traditional scientific approaches.	• There is potential for this approach to be seen as 'neither one thing nor the other'. • The inherent flexibility can lead to weak and inconclusive reports and recommendations.

Hamblin's five-stage model

Hamblin proposed a five-stage model, and it will be seen that there are clear similarities between this work and that of Kirkpatrick.

- **Level 1: Reaction.** Level 1 is evaluation conducted during, immediately after and some time after the training event, and is concerned with measuring the reaction of trainees to the training.
- **Level 2: Learning behaviour.** This level is concerned with measuring the extent to which trainees have acquired new knowledge, skills or behaviours as a result of the training event.
- **Level 3: Job behaviour.** Level 3 attempts to measure the impact of the training event on workplace performance.

- **Level 4: Functioning.** This level of evaluation is concerned with quantifying any improvement in the trainee's organization as a result of the training event, preferably expressed in cost terms.
- **Level 5: Ultimate value.** Level 5 attempts to measure any relationship between the training event and the overall success, profitability or survival of the trainee's organization.

Warr, Bird and Rackham's CIRO model

Warr, Bird and Rackham (1970) developed a four-stage model comprising:

- context evaluation;
- input evaluation;
- reaction evaluation;
- outcome evaluation.

Context evaluation involves reviewing and assessing the operational requirements for the training event and determining the individual training needs and objectives applied at three levels:

1. **Ultimate objectives.** This identifies the skills or knowledge deficit which the training event is intended to overcome.
2. **Intermediate objectives.** This quantifies the changes in workplace performance which will be necessary to overcome the deficit identified as a result of 1) above.
3. **Immediate objectives.** This identifies the new knowledge, skills or behaviour which are necessary if the trainee is to achieve the intermediate objectives.

Input evaluation involves an evaluation of the training event. This includes assessing whether or not the chosen methodology is the most appropriate means of meeting the training need and/or whether alternative means or resources could be used to equal effect.

The level of reaction evaluation is similar to Kirkpatrick's and Hamblin's Level 1 evaluation; it involves measuring the reactions of trainees both during and immediately after the training event.

The outcome evaluation level comprises four stages:

- defining the training objectives;
- selecting or constructing the evaluation tools and measures;

- using the evaluation tools and instruments;
- assessing and reviewing the results.

As we outlined above, some evaluators are keen to determine the value of training in terms of money spent and earned value, and there are two principal models for this purpose.

The Phillips five-level ROI model

With the requirement to identify the financial benefits derived from training in mind, Phillips (1995, 1996, 1997) extended Kirkpatrick's model by adding a fifth, cost–benefit stage. Phillips's model is summarized in Table 8.2.

Table 8.2   *Phillips's model of evaluation*

Level	Brief description
1. Reaction and planned action	Measures participant's reactions to the programme and outlines specific plans for implementation
2. Learning	Measures skills, knowledge or attitude change
3. Job application	Measures change in behaviour on the job and specific application of training material
4. Business results	Measures business impact of the programme
5. Return on investment	Measures the monetary values of the results and costs for the programme, usually expressed as a percentage.

While a number of organizations and training professionals have expressed some concern at being able to properly evaluate the higher levels of Kirkpatrick's or Phillips's model, there are an increasing number of examples in which more sophisticated evaluations of training have involved quantification of costs and benefits in terms of both monetary value and intangible value such as increased staff morale.

For Phillips (1997), calculating the Return on Investment (ROI) involves four distinct stages:

1. Data collection.
2. Isolating the effects of training.

3. Converting data to a monetary value.
4. Calculating the return on investment.

Each of the four stages can be applied at all five levels of the ROI five-stage model described above. In order to calculate the ROI it is necessary for the previous three stages to have been completed. For Phillips (1997) the ROI is calculated using the following formulae.

First, ROI is calculated using the programme benefits and costs. A cost–benefit ratio (CBR) is calculated by dividing the programme benefits by the programme costs. This is expressed as a formula thus:

$$CBR = \frac{\text{Programme benefits}}{\text{Programme costs}}$$

The return on investment is calculated by dividing the net benefits by the programme costs, where the net benefits are the programme benefits minus the costs. Thus the formula for ROI is:

$$ROI\ (100\%) = \frac{\text{Net programme benefits}}{\text{Programme costs}} \times 100$$

An even stronger advocate of the need to identify the costed benefits of undertaking training is Kearns (2000), who very firmly makes the case that the only training that should be supported by an organization is that which is clearly linked with the attainment of its strategic objectives. He outlines a very comprehensive 10-point added-value evaluation model:

1. Business value analysis. Identify the specific areas where there is a need for improvement and the ways in which you can generate more value from the ways in which you operate as an organization or business. Kearns is of the view that there is no need to even consider the influence of training and development at this stage.
2. People impact. Identify those individuals along the value chain who have an impact on the output measures identified during step 1.
3. Training needs analysis. Having identified those individuals who have most impact on the output measures, you now need to determine whether or not training and development is the means of improving their ability to improve performance. If training and development is not the answer, what is?

4. Measurement systems. Can we devise and implement a performance measurement system to check that we are on track to improve performance?
5. Learning objectives and design. What learning objectives can we devise which will ensure that our training and development will provide the desired performance improvement?
6. Contract. Have we devised a contract to ensure that all staff involved, including line managers, have set out their own responsibilities and are committed to the training and development?
7. Reaction. What is the reaction of the learners to the training event?
8. Learning. Are the learners learning?
9. Transfer. Are the learners transferring what they have learnt to the workplace?
10. Evaluation and feedback. Critically examine the steps taken, particularly those at 1 and 4. Have we added value to our organization? Have we learned from the experience? Have we informed our people of the results?

Think carefully about Kearns's approach. Is this model appropriate as a means of evaluating an organization's response to diversity?

Following publication of the Macpherson Report (1999), a number of organizations have been accused of being institutionally racist. Let us now apply the first four stages of Kearns's model to measuring the impact of any subsequent diversity training.

1. Business value analysis. What needs to be improved? Organizational structure? Business processes? Management style? Organizational culture? Recruitment policies? Workplace behaviour?
2. People impact. Which individuals are responsible for those processes identified in stage 1?
3. Training needs analysis. How can the performance of these individuals be improved? Is there a need for training, or can improvement be achieved in other ways?
4. Measurement systems. How do we measure the performance of these individuals to ensure that their performance has improved and that we have achieved the output specification?

EVALUATION TOOLS

Whatever the evaluation purpose, methodology or model, all evaluation processes require a set of valid and reliable tools and measures, and it is this area that is now examined. As we discussed above, evaluators can approach the evaluation study from a number of different perspectives, and the preferred school of evaluation will often influence the tools and processes used within the evaluation. Table 8.3 draws on our experience of both undertaking evaluations and having our own learning events externally evaluated:

Table 8.3   *Evaluation tools*

School	Tools and processes
Experimental	Questionnaires Structured interviews Data analysis (eg knowledge test results)
Illuminative	Participant observation Semi-structured interviews Group discussions
Systems based	Input v output analysis Training needs analysis (TNA) v outcomes analysis
Goal free	Long-term observation studies of everyone concerned with the training event
Illuminative research	Any or all of the above as agreed with the key stakeholders.

Any evaluation requires the application of valid and reliable tools, measures and processes, and in our experience the evaluation methodology should be consistent with the type of training to be evaluated. In addition to the tools mentioned in Table 8.3, we have seen evaluations make use of learning logs, repertory grids, critical incident analysis and appraisals. If you are responsible for strategy implementation, you can also make some useful links with strategic assessments and macro-evaluation processes such as Investors in People, European Foundation for Quality Management and the balanced scorecard. It is also important that the evaluator pays particular attention to the need to isolate the effects of training in order to better measure whether or not training was the cause of any change in knowledge, behaviour or skills levels.

As we noted above, a number of evaluation approaches are concerned with identifying the extent to which the training event has led to improved knowledge, skills, attitudes and workplace performance, and it is this area of assessment to which we now turn.

ASSESSMENT

Should the impact of diversity training be assessed? Of late we have found this to be one of the hottest areas of debate. On the one hand, those concerned with performance issues and ROI will argue that what gets measured gets done; on the other hand, it is argued that this area of training is very much part of personal development and that it is particularly difficult to measure attitudinal change.

Table 8.4   *Assessment processes for various learning intentions*

Learning intention	Assessment process
Increased knowledge	1. Self report 2. Multiple choice examination 3. Essay 4. Verbal question and answer 5. Line manager interview 6. Group discussion 7. Appraisal
Behaviour change	1. Role play 2. Assessment centre 3. Group discussion 4. Workplace assessment 5. Self report
Attitudinal change	1. Self report 2. Questionnaire 3. Workplace assessment 4. Group discussion

In our experience there is a very happy middle ground, and provided you are aware of some of the pitfalls you can develop a comprehensive and valid assessment scheme that provides reliable assessment data and feedback. We feel that there are a number of key principles:

- As with evaluation, assessment processes are not as scientific as some would like to portray.
- Do not rely on single assessment processes. Use a number of different approaches to validate your final assessment.
- Ensure that your processes are capable of assessing what you want to measure (eg will a knowledge check test any behavioural change?).
- Ensure that the assessment process is consistent with the learning intentions of the training event (eg if you are delivering an 'awareness course', exactly what changes are you expecting and how will they be measured?).

We have found Table 8.4 a useful way of helping to devise a comprehensive assessment process.

In our experience, assessment of any change following diversity training is particularly problematic, and we firmly believe that assessment processes must be as comprehensive as possible. This issue has been highlighted by the emergence of National Training Organizations (NTOs) and their remit to develop National Occupational Standards (NOSs) across a wide range of employment sectors. The intention here is to devise a broad range of competences which cover all of the core tasks and functions undertaken by employees in their workplace. Assessment is typically the responsibility of line managers or trained assessors, and many of the NOSs are linked to formal qualifications through National Vocational Qualifications (NVQs). While we agree that NOSs are a useful way of defining the core tasks and functions of a given profession, we are particularly concerned that this should not be seen as the only way of assessing performance and competency. For example, in dealings with someone from an ethnic minority background an employee may be able to demonstrate competency under assessment yet remain a committed racist.

PUTTING EVALUATION INTO PERSPECTIVE

A recent visit to the Personnel Today website (www.personneltoday.com) provided an interesting insight into the way in which evaluation is currently being used as a means of examining the worth of training and development and its impact on wider organizational strategic objectives.

Michael Miller reports that a recent survey undertaken by the global consulting company Accenture found that only 2 per cent of companies were able to evaluate achievement of learning objectives in line with business measures such as productivity gains, revenue growth, net income growth, decreased employee turnover and overall industry recognition.

The report found that where the business impact of learning was measured it was often done in ways that could rarely be translated into useful business metrics. In this regard Accenture recommended that companies seek to align learning initiatives to business goals and cited the following examples:

- measuring overall business impact of the learning function;
- extending learning to customers, suppliers and business partners;
- supporting their organizations' most critical competencies and jobs;
- integrating learning with functions such as talent management;
- using technology to deliver learning;
- providing leadership development courses.

A second article by Stephanie Sparrow reported on a cross-Atlantic evaluation of approaches to blended learning. The results of the first 'Transatlantic Blended Learning Survey' found that organizations in both the UK and the USA were keen to ensure that line managers took greater responsibility for transferring learning into the workplace. Additionally there was consensus in the area of individual responsibility where there were signs that participants were having to accept the onus of learning transfer themselves.

The survey did highlight differences both in terms of the application of e-learning where the use of technology in learning was more advanced in the USA and in terms of perceived effectiveness of alternative training methods. Survey respondents were asked to assess the effectiveness of different training methods. We reproduce the findings of the original report below. When listed in order of effectiveness, with the first method regarded as 'the most effective', UK respondents ranked them as follows:

- instructor-led training;
- on-the-job training;
- coaching;
- blended learning;
- learning from peers and colleagues;
- self-study methods;
- e-learning.

When compared with the UK view, it appears that North Americans have a much more positive perception of the effectiveness of blended learning. They ranked the learning methods as follows:

- blended learning;
- instructor-led training;
- on-the-job training;
- coaching;
- learning from peers;
- e-learning;
- self-study.

Respondents were also asked to assess the efficiency of different training methods where efficiency was defined as producing 'a result that is compatible with the cost and time incurred in the purchase/development and delivery'. The results also revealed cross-Atlantic differences, and differences in the most *effective* as compared with the most *efficient*, with the UK voting on-the-job-training as the most efficient and instructor-led training as the fourth most efficient method. In the USA blended and e-learning were ranked the most efficient methods.

The final article of interest outlines Andrew Mayo's work on measuring the ROI of the wider HR function. Mayo came to similar conclusions as those advanced by Miller and he was critical of the ability of HR to measure its contribution to business outcomes. For Mayo:

> The successful HR functions of today and the future must be able to measure and monitor their own effectiveness in supporting operational management and delivering services, and must also be able to justify and evaluate projects. (Mayo, 2004)

Mayo is critical of most HR programmes which he describes as comprising a series of activity-driven objectives such as introduction of training programme A or HR function Z rather than comprising strategic plans which are aligned with the attainment of business objectives.

Advocating the type of ROI exercise described above, Mayo argues that HR practitioners need to understand how the support function of HR provides value to an organization and should be able to calculate both the costs of the function and the returns HR gives back to the organization.

KEY LEARNING POINTS

In this chapter we invited you to think about the role of evaluation and assessment within a programme of diversity training.

- We noted that there are a number of approaches to evaluation and that you need to determine the approach best suited to your organization or training need.
- Generally there are four reasons for undertaking an evaluation: proving, improving, learning and controlling. It is important that you understand the reason for wishing to evaluate your training programme, as this will determine the style or school of evaluation that will be used.
- We introduced the five major schools of evaluation and invited you to determine the relative strengths and weaknesses of each approach. We invited you to look in some detail at the concept of Return on Investment and outlined a simple formula which enables you to make such a calculation.

Chapter 9

Diversity Training in Action

LEARNING INTENTIONS

Having completed this chapter, we hope that you will have:

- examined the extent to which one government department is building the capability of its staff, through training, to undertake Race Equality Impact Assessments as part its general duty under the Race Relations (Amendment) Act 2000 (RRAA);
- considered the requirements of the RRAA and assessed the degree to which your organization is meeting those requirements;
- examined the approach of one multinational private company in seeking to create a more inclusive and diverse workforce;
- considered the external factors facing the company and considered the extent to which your own organization is facing and responding to similar challenges.

INTRODUCTION

By its very definition, the major focus of this book is to explore the nature of diversity and the most appropriate means of providing training and development both in terms of individual learning requirements and those of a wider organizational perspective. This chapter takes a slightly different approach in that it examines in some detail the approaches of two very different organizations in developing diversity training programmes that are closely aligned with the achievement of strategic level objectives.

The chapter comprises two case studies that provide an opportunity to compare and contrast the approaches of one public sector and one private sector organization developing examples of diversity training programmes. The case studies describe the nature, focus and ambitions of the organizations, including the rationale underpinning their approach to diversity training, before exploring the diversity training provision. The first case study examines the approach of the Office of the Deputy Prime Minister (ODPM) in preparing its staff to meet the legal duties imposed on public authorities by the RRAA. This case study is also used as a means of exploring the RRAA in more detail and, in particular, the legal duty to undertake a Race Equality Impact Assessment of any proposed policy or policy that is subject to substantial change. The second case study explores the approach of a recently privatized utilities company, National Grid Transco (NGT), which is responding to a number of business challenges by way of an inclusion and diversity strategy.

We also hope that you will use the case studies as a means of comparing how your own organization is responding to issues similar to those identified in this chapter.

THE OFFICE OF THE DEPUTY PRIME MINISTER

The ODPM is a central government department formed in May 2002 with the responsibility for devising policy on regional and local government, planning, housing and the fire service. Additionally it is responsible for the Social Exclusion Unit, the Neighbourhood Renewal Unit and the Government Offices for the Regions. The ODPM employs some 6,500 staff, including 1,800 in its four agencies and 2,700 in the nine Government Offices for the Regions. The annual expenditure of the ODPM amounts to around £50 billion.

The ODPM has an ambitious agenda and one that cuts across several other government departments. In terms of planning and housing it aims to create sustainable communities which it describes as those that help to promote a better quality of life for all residents and that address problems such as homelessness and anti-social behaviour. As noted by the Office, 'creating sustainable communities requires good governance, public participation, partnership working and civic pride' (ODPM, 2005: 4) and in this regard ODPM plans include major investment in housing, transport and regeneration, changes in planning, design and construction and a regional approach to tackling the different housing problems across the country.

It is the belief of the ODPM that sustainable communities are the building blocks of a decent, tolerant and inclusive society. In this regard much of its work involves the regeneration of particularly deprived areas and to encourage a larger proportion of communities and individuals not previously involved in community activities to participate more freely in such activities and help to generate what the ODPM terms civic pride.

This aspect of the ODPM's work is enshrined in its publication *Sustainable Communities: Building for the future* (2003). Launched by the Deputy Prime Minister in February 2003 it provides an action plan to address a number of issues, including:

- empowering regional and local government and pushing up performance standards;
- regenerating declining communities;
- tackling social exclusion and homelessness;
- providing more high-quality affordable housing, particularly in the four growth areas in the South East of England – vital for the people who make essential services work for the community;
- making the planning system faster, fairer and more efficient, and designing attractive towns, cities and public places.

With such a wide-ranging agenda, and one which cuts across a range of diversity issues, it is vital that diversity sits at the heart of the policy-making process within the ODPM. As with almost all government departments and public authorities in England and Wales, the ODPM has both a general duty to promote race equality in the way it discharges it, functions and more specific duties in relation to its human resources function. We briefly mentioned the Race Relations (Amendment) Act 2000 in Chapter 2 and it is now timely to examine this significant piece of legislation in more detail.

The general duty

Under the Race Relations (Amendment) Act 2000 most public authorities now have a statutory general duty to promote race equality. This means they must pay due regard to the need to:

- eliminate unlawful racial discrimination;
- promote equality of opportunity; and
- promote good race relations.

The purpose of this general duty is to ensure that those organizations discharging government functions build the general duty into its policy-making processes and the way it delivers its services. For the Commission for Racial Equality (CRE) the benefits accruing to the organization in terms of policy making and service delivery include:

- encouraging policy makers to be more aware of possible problems;
- more informed decision making;
- ensuring that policies are properly targeted;
- improving the authority's ability to deliver suitable and accessible services that meet varied needs;
- encouraging greater openness about policy making;
- increasing confidence in public services, especially among ethnic minority communities.

(*Source:* www.cre.org.uk)

Specific duties

Government authorities also have specific duties to help them to meet the general duty. The specific duty is intended to provide a framework for measuring progress in equality of opportunity in public sector employment. They are intended to guide initiatives that will lead to a more representative public workforce. It should be noted that they represent the minimum standard and that other diversity issues, such as gender, disability and sexual orientation may be relevant to the pursuit of good employment practice. The duty in this regard is to monitor the numbers of staff in post and applicants for employment, training and promotion by reference to their ethnicity. Additionally those organizations employing more than 150 staff are required to monitor by reference to their ethnicity the number of staff who receive training, undergo performance assessment procedures, are involved in grievance procedures, are the subject of disciplinary procedures and whose employment has been terminated. Moreover the results of this monitoring must be published annually and all staff in the organization should receive training regarding their responsibilities in meeting the requirements of the general duty described above.

The race equality scheme

An additional specific duty for some government authorities is a requirement to publish a plan – known as a Race Equality Scheme (RES) – where it explains how the organization will end discrimination in all areas of its work.

In this regard commitment to the ODPM RES is demonstrated at the highest level as noted by the current Minister for Diversity and Parliamentary Under Secretary of State:

> We, the Office of the Deputy Prime Minister, should be at the leading edge of race equality and diversity. This is not just because of our role as a public organization, but also because of our specific responsibilities for issues of social inclusion, urban regeneration and neighbourhood renewal. (ODPM, 2003:2)

Furthermore, the current ODPM Permanent Secretary noted that:

> The Race Relations (Amendment) Act 2000 is a real opportunity to make race equality a central part of everything we do. Diversity is essential in a modern government that is committed to delivering policies effectively. (ODPM, 2003:2)

Responsibility for overseeing the response of public authorities to this ambitious agenda rests with the Commission for Racial Equality and it is worth briefly noting their specific responsibilities in this regard.

The role of the Commission for Racial Equality

Under the auspices of the Race Relations (Amendment) Act the Commission for Racial Equality (CRE) has the power to undertake two types of formal investigation in relation to the duties: a named person investigation (the named respondent will usually be an organization not an individual) and a general investigation. Furthermore it must also carry out an investigation if required to do so by the Secretary of State. The named person investigation will be instigated in cases where it is suspected that a particular company or organization is discriminating on racial grounds. General investigations do not focus on any particular company or organization; typically they will be concerned with broader areas of activity in specific areas of government policy or service delivery. This might include, for example, examining the extent to which school admissions policy is promoting good race relations or establishing whether certain professions retain discriminatory recruitment processes.

In the case of a named person investigation, if the CRE is satisfied that unlawful acts of discrimination have occurred it can issue a non-discrimination notice to the respondents, requiring them to take specified action to prevent any further discrimination and can enforce compliance with the terms of a non-discrimination notice.

Race Equality Impact Assessment

Race Equality Impact Assessment (REIA) provides a means of examining whether or not policies, processes and functions are meeting the general duty. Developed by the CRE and the Home Office in consultation with other government departments it provides a systematic process which allows organizations to decide whether or not a proposed policy is relevant to race equality and if so to ensure that such policies are unlikely to have a discriminatory impact on different racial groups. An REIA comprises two levels of assessment: initial screening and full impact assessment.

Initial screening

Initial screening involves defining the aims and objectives of the proposed functions and policies and the following questions should be applied to any proposed function or policy:

- What is the purpose of the function or proposed policy?
- Who is affected by it?
- Who is the policy intended to benefit and how?

In this way the screening enables new and proposed policies to be assessed to the extent to which they assist with:

- eliminating unlawful racial discrimination;
- promoting equality of opportunity;
- promoting good race relations between people from different racial groups.

The screening should attempt to assess the extent to which there is any evidence to show that as a result of the proposed policy:

- there will be differential impact to certain racial groups;
- racial groups have different needs or experiences in respect of the policies or functions;
- the policy or function could hinder equality of opportunity and/or damage good race relations;
- we need to go outside our normal channels of information to find evidence for the initial screening to help reach an informed decision.

If the answer to any of the above questions is yes, then the policy should be subject to a full impact assessment.

Full impact assessment

As can be seen in Figure 9.1, a full impact assessment comprises eight components, each of which provides a systematic means of further

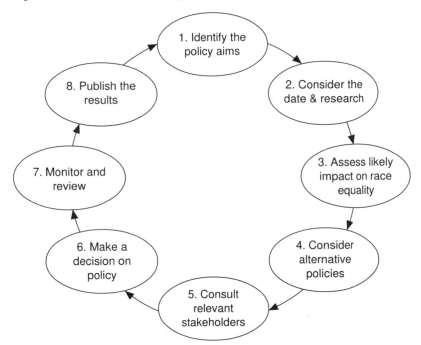

Figure 9.1 *Race Equality Impact Assessment (full impact assessment)*

exposing the extent to which the policy is likely to meet the requirements of the general duty.

As can be seen, the third stage of this process provides an opportunity to drill down into the policy and make a judgement as to the extent to which the policy might prevent the organization from complying with the general duty. Specifically this stage of the process will involve questions such as:

- Is there an adverse impact on any racial group in respect of either the quantitative or qualitative data?
- Could the way the policy is carried out have an adverse impact on
  - equality of opportunity of some racial groups?
  - good relations between different racial groups?
- Does the policy promote equality of opportunity and/or good race relations?
- Is the policy directly or indirectly discriminatory, and if so in the case of the latter, can it be justified?
- Is the policy intended to increase equality of opportunity by permitting positive action to redress disadvantage, and if so is it lawful?
- Is further research or consultation necessary?
- Would this additional work be proportionate in respect of the importance of the proposed policy?

The process is designed to be challenging and is one which requires policy makers to look long and hard at the aims of the policy and ascertain the extent to which policies can proactively improve race relations and prevent discrimination. Given the constantly changing agenda, both in terms of the issues facing governments in the 21st century and the nature of diversity, designing an effective training intervention provided a number of challenges. First there was a need to equip practitioners with the necessary knowledge, understanding and skills to be able to effectively undertake an REIA. Secondly there was a need to ensure that staff at all levels of the organization were aware of their responsibilities under the new legislation.

The ODPM Training Programme

The initial commission for training ODPM staff was set at four levels and reflected the general and specific duties defined within the RRAA as follows:

1. A *Board Level Workshop* was intended to raise awareness of the most senior members of staff as to the strategic requirements of the RRAA and the ways in which this would impact on policies being developed within the ODPM and its internal HR processes. The workshop was designed so as to enable board members to discuss the strategic implications of the Act, how this would interface with business planning processes and how implementation would be addressed across internal departments.

2. *HR Workshops*: These workshops were specifically designed for HR professionals and were similar in approach to the policy-level seminars described below. The key focus here was to ensure that race equality is an integral part of the HR function within the ODPM. The case study was built around ODPM internal processes, including recruitment, appraisal and promotion.

3. *Policy Level Workshop*. This training focused on how impact assessments were to be built into the policy-making process and was specifically concerned with enabling delegates to devise more effective and inclusive policy. Delegates were taught key aspects of the relevant legislation affecting race and diversity issues and examined detailed case studies to develop their understanding of the REIA process. The training also takes account of how these impact assessments are aligned with other areas of good practice and policy-making processes such as Regulatory Impact Assessments and the Cabinet Office guidance on stakeholder consultation. The case study utilized statistical data on a range of issues that are pertinent to the work of the ODPM, including population distribution across England and Wales in terms of age, occupation and qualifications by ethnic group and religion or belief (see www.cre.gov.uk. or www.statistics.gov.uk).

4. *Staff Briefing*. The briefing sessions were designed to ensure that all ODPM staff were aware of the Race Equality Scheme, the response of the ODPM and how Race Equality is placed at the heart of ODPM work and its policies. This training was designed to ensure that the ODPM meets the statutory requirement under the RRAA to train all staff in the legislation.

Further developments

A recent initiative has been to develop a more inclusive Diversity Impact Assessment for policy makers to take account of broader issues such as age, disability, gender and sexual orientation. In this regard additional demographic data were acquired from the Office of National Statistics, the Equal Opportunities Commission and Stonewall (see www.statistics.gov.uk, www.eoc.org.uk and www.stonewall.org.uk). In many ways this was a natural development both in terms of alignment with plans to bring together the Commission for Race Equality, the Equal Opportunities Commission and the Disability Rights Commission within a new Commission for Equality and Human Rights (see www.womenandequalityunit.gov.uk) and initiatives such as the Equality Standard for Local Government (see www.lg-employers.gov.uk). Moreover there was anecdotal evidence that earlier impact assessments that had focused on race were identifying the impact of policy initiatives in other areas of diversity such as religion and sexual orientation.

Evaluating the ODPM programme

At the time of writing, a full evaluation has yet to be undertaken; end-of-course questionnaires do indicate that delegates (particularly policy makers and HR specialists) have found the programme to be particularly useful and relevant to their work. Whilst the more detailed levels of evaluation (as described in Chapter 8) are likely to provide more meaningful evidence, such as the impact on individual workplace and wider organizational performance, two areas are worthy of further note. First, the workshops are solely concerned with improving delegates knowledge and understanding of the impact assessment process; there is an assumption that delegates will already be aware of the requirements of the Race Relations Act 1976 and the nature of prejudice and discrimination. Secondly, successful implementation of a scheme such as this requires knowledge, understanding and support at every level of the organization. It is vitally important that the leaders of an organization understand what is required at the middle management level and equally important that those engaged in front-line delivery understand and support policy and management decisions.

1. How do you assess the impact of your policies or strategies on different ethnic groups?	
2. Do you take into account the impact of such policies or strategies on other groups within the community (eg with reference to gender, disability, age or sexual orientation)?	
3. Does your organization monitor its HR policies and functions (eg recruitment, promotion, training or pay) with a view to ascertaining whether or not these policies might be discriminatory?	
4. To what extent does your organization build anti-discriminatory measures into aspects of service delivery?	
5. Does your organization incorporate anti-discriminatory measures into organizational processes such as procurement?	
6. If your organization does respond positively to the issues raised in questions 1 to 5 above, what training does it provide and to whom is the training provided?	

Figure 9.2   *Consider the above in respect of your own organization.*

NATIONAL GRID TRANSCO

National Grid Transco (NGT) was established in 2002 following the merger of National Grid and Lattice. Lattice was the holding company of Transco which had itself been created following the privatization of British Gas in 1986 and a de-merger which created two separate companies: BG plc and Centrica. Transco became part of BG plc and in

1999 a plc in its own right — BG Transco plc (see www.ngtgroup.com and www.transco.co.uk).

Within the UK, Transco is the largest utility company, with a staff of 24,500 generating £2.2 billion profit from a turnover of £9 billion (figures correct at 31 March 2004 and taken from www.ngtgroup.com/about/mn_facts.html). With a customer base of 21 million in the UK, NGT has an equally impressive record in the United States, where it delivers electricity to 3.3 million customers and gas to a further 560,000.

As with many global companies, NGT pays particular attention to corporate government responsibilities and has created a number of committees including Audit, Executive, Finance, Nominations, Remuneration and Risk & Responsibility, all of which report directly to the Board.

NGT has also set out a public statement outlining a Framework for Responsible Business and its Behavioural Values. These are underpinned by a number of principal policies supported by definitions of functional responsibilities, procedures, standards and compliance arrangements. Policy areas which are openly available on the NGT website include safety and occupational health, environment, employee ethics, confidentiality, whistleblower protection and human resources.

1. How do you assess the impact of your policies or strategies on different ethnic groups?	
2. Does your organization make its policies openly available to competitor organizations?	

Figure 9.3   *Policy comparison: Consider the above*

Of particular interest in the context of diversity is the HR policy and the Board is keen to emphasize the degree of independence with which individual businesses can operate within their respective market sectors. However, in respect of the HR policy, NGT are keen that individual business units develop supporting policies which have coherency, have relevance to Group-wide policies and are developed in a way which supports prime corporate objectives.

From an organization-wide perspective, the policy framework sets out that NGT is committed to:

- being an equal opportunities employer encouraging diversity and avoiding any discrimination on the grounds of race, colour, religion, political opinion, nationality, gender, disability, sexual orientation, age, social origin and status, indigenous status or other status unrelated to the individual's ability to perform his or her work;
- promoting a work environment free from any harassment, intimidation or bullying;
- developing reward and recognition schemes that will allow National Grid Transco businesses to recruit, retain and motivate its employees in a way that reflects the market in which they operate;
- relevant consultation with employees and their representatives;
- fostering a learning environment to enable employees to realize their full potential.

(National Grid Transco, 2002)

For NGT, the HR policy remains the responsibility of the Group HR Director, as does the responsibility for ensuring compliance throughout the Group. Each of the associate companies within the NGT Group

1. To what extent does your organization allow individual business units to develop local policies?	
2. If the responsibility for HR policy is devolved, what checks and balances are in place to ensure that local policies are aligned with corporate policy?	
3. Is the responsibility for training centrally managed or managed at a local level?	
4. What are the respective strengths and weaknesses of adopting a central responsibility for training and when delegating authority to a local level?	

Figure 9.4   *Central responsibility and delegated authority*

must ensure that they work within the Group Policy Framework and report such compliance on an annual basis, with the Group Executive providing an annual report on corporate performance in this area.

The NGT Valuing People through Inclusion Initiative

In 2005 NGT announced a new diversity initiative named 'Valuing People through Inclusion' by writing to all employees enclosing an information pack and forwarding this correspondence to their home addresses. The initiative is championed by a Group Director and the rationale underpinning the strategy is made clear throughout the literature and includes drivers such as the need for NGT to identify and recruit talented staff and to develop within the organization an inclusive and supportive culture. This latter aspect is particularly important given the history and heritage of the company. In our experience this is a significant issue and one that is often overlooked both by private sector companies involved in mergers and acquisitions and public sector organizations involved in major departmental change.

The case for this particular initiative is particularly compelling. As argued by the Trades Union Congress (TUC), there will be a greater demand for flexible working patterns both on the part of workers as well as employees. The TUC also notes that it is likely that the provision of part-time working opportunities will need to grow; however, with the current trends of full-time employment likely to remain generally stable, it is this latter area of employment that will require more innovative thinking, particularly taking into account the increased need for workplace flexibility and the emerging trends and current employment data.

- Over the past 10 years the number of employee jobs has increased by 2 million, whilst self-employed jobs have declined by quarter of a million.
- In the next 10 years it is predicted that employee jobs will grow by another 2 million and that self-employment will continue to decline.
- Of the 2 million jobs, it is estimated that around two-thirds will be undertaken by women and that around two-thirds of all the new jobs will be part-time (it is estimated that the 1.5 million part-time jobs will be split equally between men and women).
- By 2010 it is estimated that more than four-fifths of male employees and over half of women employees will still be working full-time.

- It is estimated that nearly 3 million new jobs will be created in the services sector (both private and public).

Source: http://www.tuc.org.uk/changingtimes/worktrends.htm

The changing nature of employment and workplace flexibility and the importance of valuing people through inclusion are further highlighted by demographic data produced by the National Research Guidance Forum (www.guidance-research.org). This website provides demographic, statistical and forecast data across a range of employment sectors and in respect of the utilities market sector the need for a strategy such as that developed by NGT is clear.

In respect of gender balance, the energy and utility sector remains a predominantly male-dominated workforce, with male employees making up 74 per cent of the workforce in the sector as compared to 54 per cent in the whole UK economy. Whilst Figure 9.5 predicts that the overall number of employees is likely to continue to fall during the current decade, it also appears to suggest that the current 75:25 ratio of men to women employees may be replaced by one which is more reflective of the current national figure.

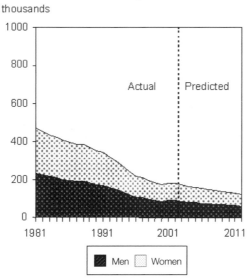

Source: www.national-guidance.org

Figure 9.5   *Changing patterns of gender in utilities, 1981–2011*

In terms of ethnicity very little information is available concerning the proportion of individual ethnic minorities groups employed within the utilities sector. However, the data do indicate that the workforce is predominantly white, with about 97 per cent categorized as of White European origin, compared to 93 per cent in the whole economy. However, it is interesting to note that 20 per cent of staff employed in call centres within the gas and water industry are from an ethnic minority background.

However, with the majority of utilities sector workers reaching retirement age in the next decade, it is the ageing of the workforce that has been identified as one of the most urgent labour issues the industry faces. In this regard the data indicates that 29 per cent of the total utilities sector workforce are aged 35 to 44 and a further 35 per cent are aged over 45.

The National Research Guidance Forum also notes that only 11 per cent of the workers in the sector are aged between 16 and 25 and that the age profile problem is at its most acute in the area of gas installers.

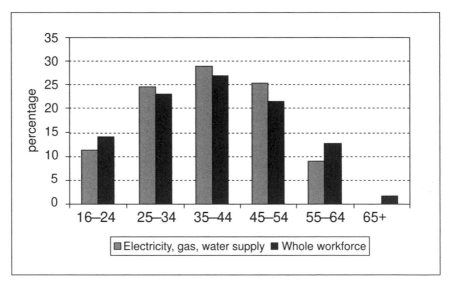

Source: www.guidance-research.org

Figure 9.6   *Age distribution in the electricity, gas and water supply sector, 2003–2004*

Taking into account the demographic trends described above, will the market sector in which you work experience similar challenges? Consider the following in respect of your own organization.

1. Can you predict times at which you will be required to recruit larger than normal numbers of new staff?	
2. Will the gender profile of your organization change during the current decade?	
3. How are you preparing current members of staff in respect of forthcoming change?	
4. Go to the National Research Guidance Forum website and establish the current position in your own employment sector.	

Figure 9.7 *Employment challenges facing your organization*

Evaluating the initiative

This initiative is very much in its infancy and it is clear that the company faces a number of challenges before the aims of the initative can be achieved. At the time of writing, the overall has yet to be translated into a more detailed training and development strategy. However, there is much to commend the approach thus far, for example in Chapter 2 we noted that the successful implementation of diversity initiatives and training programmes requires support at the highest levels in the organization. In this regard the involvement of a Group Director is seen to be crucially important. It is also important that employees at every level of the organization understand the reasons behind the initiative and can identify how the programme will impact on individual roles and responsibilities. By clearly setting out the business case for Valuing People Through Inclusion and by stating in clear concise language what the initiative stands for it is likely that more employees will both understand and support the programme. It is also important that all staff can identify the positive outcomes of such an initiative and how those outcomes relate to operational practice and success.

KEY LEARNING POINTS

In this chapter we provided two detailed case studies in order to identify how the two selected organizations have approached a programme of diversity training. In many ways there are some obvious differences between the two organizations, the drivers for the training programme and the selected strategies. The first case study has given us the opportunity to examine how a large central government department is responding to a legal duty and providing a training programme as a means of increasing staff knowledge and capability. The second case study focuses on a global company and its use of a diversity strategy to drive an organization-wide cultural change programme and to prepare for perceived future recruitment difficulties. However, the two approaches also present some areas of consensus as follows:

- Both approaches have support at the highest levels; Ministerial level in the case of the ODPM and Board level in the case of NGT.
- Both approaches are in some way influenced by external factors; for the ODPM compliance with a legal duty and a desire to create a new corporate culture and to improve its ability to recruit a more flexible and diverse workforce.
- It is also the case that both organizations are using this programme as a means of meeting much wider strategic aims. For the ODPM the desired outcomes are around developing and implementing better and more effective policy making, thus helping to achieve government aims for a more inclusive and cohesive society. In the case of NGT its strategy appears to be an integral component of a much broader corporate strategy involving business growth, profitability and organizational responsiveness in an increasingly competitive market.

As well as learning from the two case studies from a training implementation perspective we also hope that the following have added to your learning:

- The opportunity to explore in more detail the requirements of the Race Relations (Amendment) Act 2000 and the processes involved in undertaking Race Equality Impact Assessments.
- The chance to identify the recruitment and retention issues facing organizations during the next decade and beyond.
- The opportunity to reflect on your organization, its level of commitment to diversity, its response to a number of a current issues and its ability to implement effective diversity training responses.

Chapter 10

Useful Models for Diversity Training

In this chapter we present some of the models we have found useful in the context of diversity training. As with all models, they should not be used in inappropriate contexts, or if the trainer does not understand the underpinning rationale. It is far better (for the learners as well as the trainer) to try and see a model being used by someone else rather than launching into using it for the first time. Having said that, we use models to:

- help learners to see the relationship between key variables;
- analyse different aspects of diversity;
- enrich the process of learning and understanding;
- provide variation in the teaching situation;
- help people whose learning style favours 'visualizing';
- assist our own explanations of key concepts.

No model should be regarded as providing the complete story, nor should it be presented without the opportunity for discussion and challenge.

In summary, the models in this chapter are:

- group dynamics: Tuckman's Model;
- the Integration of Cultures;
- Allport's Scale of Prejudice;
- Betari's Box;
- the Paradigm of Prejudice;
- Johari's Window;

- models for analysis:
  - SWOT
  - PESTEL
  - Five Whys

GROUP DYNAMICS: TUCKMAN'S MODEL

This relates to the way individuals may behave when they come together as a group for the first time or when a group is faced with a new or challenging task such as diversity training. The model is useful both for understanding how a group you may be working with is responding, and also as a way of helping participants to understand group dynamics in their professional contexts.

Tuckman (1965) devised a five-stage model of group dynamics that has much relevance to the ways in which groups of people operate, particularly when challenged to work with the concepts found in diversity. We have found the model especially useful as a means of monitoring a group's development when managing a group which contains individuals who are resistant to change. However, it should not be seen as an inevitable path that will be followed by all groups: some groups, for example, will already have developed mature relationships and ways of working, and will not need to go through the forming and norming stage (below). The model comprises five stages:

- forming;
- storming;
- norming;
- performing;
- mourning.

Forming

When individuals meet together for a common purpose they will undertake a process of group forming. The group will generally be dependent on the course facilitator, tutor or trainer for direction and leadership. Individuals will generally be polite and conversations will be about safe and non-controversial topics. If set a task, the group will normally comply with the request. During this stage, individuals may well be testing out levels of trust within the group and will be looking for the support of like-minded members of the group. The duration of this stage will be dependent on the nature of the tasks, the expectations of group members, and the direction and tasks set by the course leader. Ice-breaking exercises will typically help the forming stage for a group.

Storming

Once the group has formed it may well move to a stage of storming, during which individuals in the group may begin to make power bids as a means of becoming a spokesperson or group leader. Hidden agendas might surface, cliques might form, and some of the more timid group members might withdraw from the process. During this stage, our experience is that individuals, and sometimes the whole group, might become quite challenging and the credibility and authority of the course leader may be questioned. The duration of this stage may be dependent on the strength of the cliques and any subsequent power plays, as well as the skill of the course leader to facilitate the group through this stage.

Norming

During this stage the group will start to develop more of a team identity and a more inclusive approach to the completion of tasks. Norming may also include a perceptible attitude change as group members become more independent and constructive. Workload will be shared and individuals will begin to identify and accept their roles within the group. Cliques will begin to dissipate. This stage can be relatively short, depending on the dynamics of the group and whether there was any significant fallout during the storming stage.

Performing

As the identity of the group and its collective spirit grows, its performance, productivity and effectiveness will increase. The group will have developed interdependence and a sense of group loyalty, creativity will be encouraged and rewarded, and disagreement will be accepted if supported by rational argument. The group members will typically be supportive of each other and most of the focus of the group will be on the achievement of the task. Performing is likely to be the longest stage of the process. More resistant groups are likely to need a higher level of facilitator intervention than top-performing groups, who will benefit from a 'hands-off' approach.

Mourning

When a group has achieved its purpose for coming together (very often the end of the course or learning event) it may well go through a stage of mourning, though in this context we see mourning as a positive rather than negative process. The group will want to celebrate success, and as the group disbands there will be a need for individuals to say their goodbyes and move on.

Whilst Tuckman's model suggests a sequential development of group dynamics, our experience is that there are a number of variables that can intervene to cause a group to regress to a previous stage. These include:

- introduction of a new member to the group;
- a group member leaving for some reason;
- a new group leader;
- a new and more challenging task;
- a change in the working environment.

THE INTEGRATION OF CULTURES

We have found this to be particularly useful when exploring the concept of integration, particularly in respect of the relationship between majority and minority groups. Integration has been at the heart of many recent debates concerning the relationship between members of majority groups and members of minority groups. At issue here is a complex series of issues relating to what some people see as 'mainstream British culture', and how members of minority groups can maintain traditional attitudes, values and beliefs. Most famously exposed by Lord Norman Tebbit's 'cricket test' (very simply, if you are born in England, regardless of your ethnic origins you should support the England cricket team), it is now at the fore of the recent debate on tightening legislation affecting immigration and asylum. As stated above, this is a particularly complex area and one which attracts a great deal of irrational thinking. We have found the following model a useful and enlightening way of describing how different cultures and communities can relate to one another.

The model can also be applied to examine interrelations between different groups within an organization, for example the relationships within a company between heterosexual and homosexual employees, and able and disabled employees.

The basis of the model (National Police Training, 2001) is to look at how two different groups of people relate to one another. Thus the base model has two categories as shown in Figure 10.1.

Figure 10.1 *Isolation with parity*

Isolation

If the two groups operate in isolation they have little or no contact with one another or, as a result of conflict, have decided to detach themselves from one another (for example, Israel and Palestine). This is also known as separatism (see Figure 10.2).

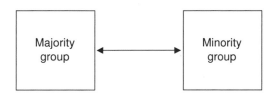

Figure 10.2 *Isolation*

Interrelation

In this relationship the two groups operate alongside one another and interconnect within the wider society while retaining their distinct identity. It is often referred to as pluralism (see Figure 10.3).

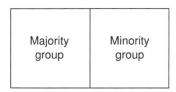

Figure 10.3 *Interrelation*

Incorporation

In this relationship, groups living together lose their individual identity and merge together to form a single and wholly assimilated identity. This is also known as fusion (see Figure 10.4).

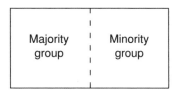

Figure 10.4 *Incorporation*

The models above have assumed that each of the groups has an equal share of power. When a power dimension is applied we can see a very different picture. This dimension applies to the relative power of the majority group and the relative power of the minority group, as shown in Figure 10.5.

Figure 10.5 *A more powerful and less powerful group*

When we apply the power or dominance factor to the three approaches of isolation, interrelation and incorporation, we find the relationships shown in Figures 10.6 and 10.7.

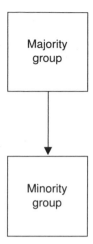

Figure 10.6 *Exclusion*

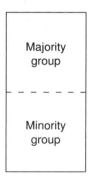

Figure 10.7 *Assimilation*

A brief review of modern history provides examples of numerous attempts by majority groups to exert domination over minority groups with the intention or outcome of excluding a minority group. The treatment of Jews by Nazi Germany in the build-up to and during the Second World War, the Apartheid system imposed in South Africa and more recent events in Bosnia are examples of an enforced exclusion of the minority group by the majority group.

In Figure 10.3 we can see that in a pluralist or interrelationist society the majority and minority groups retain their own religions, culture and language as well as their values, attitudes and traditions. In a power relationship (see Figure 10.6) the majority group will attempt to dominate the relationship and try to force the minority group to assume all of the majority group's cultural aspects.

Assimilation occurs when the minority group acquires many of the cultural aspects of the majority group and dispenses with its traditional values, attitudes and cultural norms. The power effect here is quite discrete in that the minority group can feel pressurized to accept the majority norms in order to be accepted.

ALLPORT'S SCALE OF PREJUDICE

Despite being quite dated, Allport's 1954 work on prejudice still resonates with contemporary experience. Groups that we work with still find it a helpful way of seeing how prejudice can develop. The antilocution level in the scale is a particularly powerful way of opening up a discussion about the role of language in treating people fairly.

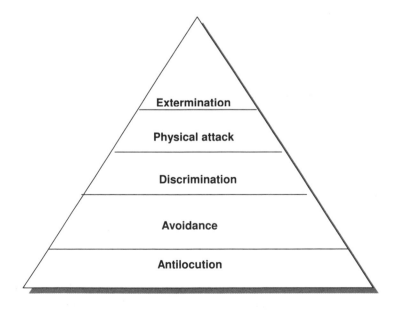

Figure 10.8 *Allport's scale of prejudice*

Gordon Allport developed a five-point hierarchical scale to describe how prejudice could be expressed. While Allport's work was directed towards what he termed 'ethnic prejudice', you will see that his model can be applied across the whole range of diversity issues.

The validity of any theoretical model is the applicability it has in respect of historical or current events. His model is expressed in Figure 10.8 above. The significance of this model is the nature of its hierarchy and the subsequent inference that the very worst outcomes of prejudice could be prevented if some attention were directed towards the first two levels. Allport also looked at the effects of discrimination on victims, and here his starting point was to identify who the victim felt was responsible for the discrimination. He argued that all victims of prejudice suffer from a level of frustration induced by discrimination. This was followed by sensitization and concern. If the victim blamed the outside world for the discrimination (whether society or an individual), he or she might respond in the following ways:

- obsessive concern or suspicion;
- cunning;
- strengthening in-group relationships;
- prejudice against other groups;
- aggression and revolution.

If victims blamed themselves for the discrimination, Allport suggested that they might exhibit the following:

- denial of group membership;
- withdrawal and passivity;
- clowning or joining in with the joke;
- self-hate;
- neuroticism.

As we noted above, the veracity of any model is whether or not it relates to live situations. The exercise below offers a suggested way of getting group participants to think through the implications of Allport's work.

Exercise

1. In respect of the five-stage hierarchy, try to think of examples from recent events that, as a result of prejudice, might amount to (or be the equivalent of):

- antilocution;
- avoidance;
- discrimination;
- aggression;
- extermination.

2. In respect of your own workplace can you think of any incidents where the victim of prejudice has:

- denied their group membership (whether this be based on ethnicity, sexuality, gender, age, physical ability or class)?
- withdrawn from the wider group membership?
- joined in with inappropriate jokes?

3. What would your response be if you found that any of your co-workers had taken any of the actions described in 2 above?

BETARI'S BOX

This simple model demonstrates the relationship between attitudes and behaviour, and how the behaviour of one individual could influence the behaviour and attitudes of others. Based on the assumption that attitudes and behaviour are linked, Betari's Box provides a vehicle for discussing the way in which people can get locked into a cycle of attitudes breeding behaviour.

The power of the Betari model is both its simplicity and its relevance. There are a number of factors in relation to the model that are significant:

- In respect of diversity training this emphasizes the need for trainers to act as effective role models or 'walk the talk'.
- It facilitates discussion about the relationship between attitudes and behaviour and the extent to which they are linked.
- It helps to stimulate discussion about the importance of interpersonal relationships in responding to diversity.

THE PARADIGM OF PREJUDICE

This model is frequently used in diversity training as a way of helping people to understand how prejudice operates. It identifies the different ways in

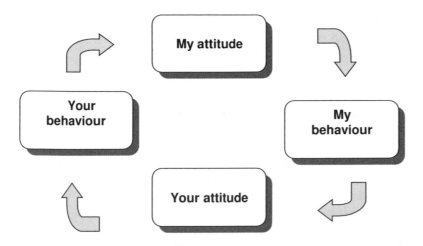

Figure 10.9 *Betari's Box*

which people may operationalize their attitudes towards a particular issue in diversity, ranging from being a prejudiced discriminator through to a non-prejudiced non-discriminator.

The model can be applied to any issue of diversity and can be used as follows:

- to help learners establish their own position on a particular diversity issue;
- to establish how individuals may occupy a range of positions on different issues;

Prejudiced discriminator	Prejudiced non-discriminator
Non-prejudiced discriminator	Non-prejudiced non-discriminator

Figure 10.10 *The paradigm of prejudice*

- to identify what movement is needed to move to the position of being a non-prejudiced non-discriminator.

JOHARI'S WINDOW

Developed by Joe Luft and Harry Ingram (hence Johari) this model helps to clarify the relationship between self-disclosure and feedback (Boshear and Albrecht, 1977). The model provides a way of thinking through how others see us and how we see ourselves. We have found this model useful in helping people to realize that there are areas of attitude and self-awareness that need to be expanded if we are to fully know ourselves. It is based in the old psychological notion that when two people are in a room there are actually six people there – me as I see myself, you as I see you, and me as you see me.

The public self represents what we know about ourselves and what others know about us. It can be such things as observable behaviour, or attitudes and values that I know I hold and that I have revealed to others.

The blind self represents things about me that others know but I am not aware of. In terms of diversity training, frequent examples of this would be the language that people use — such as being unaware of the frequent use of gender exclusionary language. An important way of dealing with the blind self is to obtain regular feedback on behaviour.

The private self represents things that I know about myself — for example prejudices that I hold but I choose not to reveal to others. Many people will claim in diversity training that their private self is private and therefore people do not have a right to know what areas it encompasses. Whilst the rights of people to maintain a private self need to be upheld, this should not deflect facilitators from engaging with people to help them confront facets of their behaviour and attitudes that may need to be dealt with.

The unknown area can of course remain enigmatic. You don't know this about me and neither do I. You don't know what you don't know. Exposure to the variation of ideas and culture that diversity implies will help to diminish this area.

Johari's Window, if used as a model and particularly if it is used in conjunction with a self-awareness exercise of some sort, is only really suitable for a skilled and experienced facilitator. When people begin to realize that they have areas of their lives that they might find disturbing, it is not uncommon for the process to expose vulnerability and deep-felt emotion. This will need to be handled with skill and sensitivity.

	Known to self	Not known to self
Known to others	The Public Self	The Blind Self
Not Known to others	The Private Self	The Unknown Area

Figure 10.11 *Johari's Window*

MODELS FOR ANALYSIS

Most training courses, and particularly diversity training, will at some stage require analysis of some issue or other. It is very helpful for trainers to have a number of analysis models available to use as the needs of the group dictate. In this section we review three models for analysis that we frequently use: SWOT analysis (www.businesslink.gov.uk), PESTEL analysis (www.businesslink.gov.uk) and Five Whys (www.portal.modern.nhs.uk). What these mean and how we use them are explained below.

SWOT

This analysis model is simply a way of taking an issue and assessing the:

Strengths

Weaknesses

Opportunities

Threats

Strengths	Focus on equality Clarity of direction Compliance with the law
Weaknesses	Too detailed Poorly communicated Confusing
Opportunities	Elimination of unlawful discrimination Reputation of the organization Identification of good practice
Threats	Lack of commitment by ordinary staff Perception of unfairness on the majority Words not translated into action

Figure 10.12 *Example of a diversity SWOT analysis*

. . . that are implicit in the issue. For example, if we wanted to analyse the effectiveness of a particular organization's Race Equality Scheme we might develop the following:

PESTEL

Like SWOT, PESTEL provides a means of analysing an issue from a range of perspectives:

Political

Economic

Social

Technological

Environmental

Legal

For example, in a training course we might want to explore and analyse a diversity policy from a range of different perspectives. It might look (in simplified form) like this:

Political	Conforms with government imperatives on diversity (White paper)
Economic	Effective recruiting – best talent Reduced costs through retention of staff The business case for diversity
Social	Elimination of unlawful discrimination The ethical case for diversity
Technological	Needs of disabled people – effective use of IT ICT issues surrounding communication of the policy
Environmental	(Strictly speaking would refer to green issues, etc.) Working environment improved Inter- and intra-personal relationships enhanced
Legal	Compliance with anti-discrimination legislation Reduction in Employment Tribunal costs Rights and responsibilities

Figure 10.13 *Example of a diversity PESTEL analysis*

Five Whys

This is a very simple model that can easily be used spontaneously in response to an issue and needs no preparation. It simply uses the question 'Why?' to drill down into an issue. Below is a simplified example of how it might be used.

Participant – 'I don't think the grievance procedure works.'

Facilitator – 'Why?'

Participant – 'People don't have confidence in it.'

Facilitator – 'Why?'

Participant – 'Because some people feel they become double victims.'

Facilitator – 'Why?'

Participant — 'They are made into a scapegoat because they have made a complaint.'

Facilitator — 'Why?'

Participant — 'Because managers don't seem to know the purpose of the procedure or how to work it properly.'

Facilitator — 'Why?'

Participant — 'I think it because some managers need more training and others have a poor attitude towards support.'

There are many other models that could be used in diversity training but those shown above are the ones we use most frequently. It is important to remember that models are not an end in themselves but a means to open up discussion and help people to understand the issues in a structured way. A good tip for any diversity training is to have a range of models pre-prepared on Microsoft Power-Point slides, OHP slides or even flipcharts. You may not have planned to use them all, but as the discussion develops and groups move into areas that they need to explore deeper, the models can be used spontaneously as the learning needs of the group dictate.

Glossary

It is useful to examine and develop an understanding of some of the terms commonly used in diversity training, as in other areas within the field of education, training and development, particularly since diversity training is constantly evolving. What follows is not a definitive list; indeed it would be presumptuous to suggest that new ideas and concepts will not be developed in the future. Rather, we have attempted here to describe the most commonly used terms in order to demystify what can be a complex body of knowledge.

Attitude Derived from an individual's values, an attitude typically reflects a tendency to react to certain events in certain ways and to approach or avoid those events that confirm or challenge the individual's values. Attitudes also affect individual beliefs and behaviour.

Behaviour Subject to a number of competing views by psychologists as to the cause of behaviour, it is generally accepted that behaviour takes the form of some kind of observable action.

Beliefs A cognitive process that involves the acceptance of some information. Beliefs can be placed within a hierarchy ranging from an opinion to a conviction.

Culture Collective knowledge, belief, art, morals, customs and any other capabilities and habits acquired by members of society.

Discrimination Unequal treatment of an individual or group of persons on the basis of features such as race, sexuality, gender or physical disposition.

Diversity Diversity is usually thought of in terms of obvious attributes: age differences, race, gender, physical ability, sexual orientation, religion and language. Increasingly it also embraces background, professional experience, skills and specialization, values and culture, and social class.

Ethnocentrism A view of the world where an individual's group is seen as the centre of everything and all other groups are measured (normally negatively) against it.

Homophobia   Literally a fear of homosexuals, it is generally used to describe the prejudice of a heterosexual person against a homosexual person on the basis of the latter's sexuality.

Labelling   Normally the result of stereotyping, labelling involves the attachment of a certain label (usually a negative attribute) to a group of people.

Positive action   Positive action (although not a legally defined term) is permissible and includes actions on the part of employers to encourage members of under-represented groups to apply for job vacancies within the organization. Positive action is designed to promote equal access to opportunities for employment up to the point of selection. It does not permit discrimination to take place during the selection process. As such it is permissible for organizations to set targets but unlawful for them to set quotas.

Positive discrimination   Positive discrimination is unlawful. It could include actions such as discriminating against members of a specific racial group in order to increase the presence of a minority racial group as a means of redressing the balance.

Prejudice   Prejudice can take a number of forms. As an attitude it involves a negative disposition taken towards a group of persons, based on a negative perception of traits that are assumed to be present within all members of that group. As behaviour it relates to the unequal treatment of an individual or group based on a negative perception of the presumed qualities of the group to which the individual belongs.

Racism   A prejudice that is founded on the basis of race, in which other races to one's own are seen as inferior.

Sexism   A prejudice based on a person's gender in which the other gender is seen as inferior.

Stereotyping   A cognitive process that leads to a generalization concerning the characteristics of a group of people.

Values   A general set of principles that have been developed within a culture and that are seen as having prominence within the culture.

Selected Websites

The internet has become an increasingly useful resource in relation to diversity over the part few years. The following are a selection of websites that we have used in support of diversity training. There are, of course, many thousands of other potentially useful sites that can be accessed using the main search engines.

Civil Service — Diversity: What Works: www.diversity-whatworks.gov.uk

Billed as the 'Civil Service Diversity website' this resource contains a great deal of information about good practice in relation to diversity in the public sector. The site is managed by the Cabinet Office. Entries range from age to work–life balance, and there are many useful case studies of what works in responding to diversity.

Commission for Racial Equality: www.cre.gov.uk

The Commission for Racial Equality is a publicly funded, non-governmental body set up under the Race Relations Act 1976 to tackle racial discrimination and promote racial equality. It works in both the public and private sectors to encourage fair treatment and to promote equal opportunities for everyone, regardless of their race, colour, nationality, or national or ethnic origin.

- It provides information and advice to people who think they have suffered racial discrimination or harassment.
- It works with public bodies, businesses and organizations from all sectors to promote policies and practices that will help to ensure equal treatment for all.

- It runs campaigns to raise awareness of race issues, and encourage organizations and individuals to play their part in creating a just society.
- It makes sure that all new laws take full account of the Race Relations Act and the protection it gives against discrimination.

Disability Rights Commission: www.drc-gb.org

The stated goal of the Disability Rights Commission is 'a society where all disabled people can participate fully as equal citizens'.

Established in April 2000, the Commission, in common with the other main agencies, focuses on the elimination of discrimination against disabled people and promotes their equality of opportunity. Its website contains a great deal of useful information and resources.

The Equal Opportunities Commission: www.eoc.org.uk

The Equal Opportunities Commission is the leading agency working to eliminate sex discrimination in 21st century Britain. It is campaigning to:

- close the pay gap between women and men;
- make it easier for parents to balance work with family responsibilities;
- increase the number of women in public life;
- break free of male and female stereotypes;
- end sexual harassment at work;
- make public services relevant to the differing needs of men and women;
- secure comprehensive equality legislation in Europe, England, Scotland and Wales.

Lesbian and Gay Employment Rights: www.lager.dircon.co.uk

Lesbian and Gay Employment Rights (LAGER) is an independent organization to help lesbians and gay men who are experiencing problems at work or while looking for work. Problems in this area can arise because of direct or indirect discrimination on the grounds of sexuality. LAGER can provide help, support and advice to lesbians and gay men who are discriminated against on the grounds of race, gender, disability, age, HIV status, pregnancy or marital status.

Royal Association for Disability and Rehabilitation: www.radar.org.uk

The Royal Association for Disability and Rehabilitation is a national organization of and for disabled people. Its key areas of activity are:

- supporting over 500 local and national disability organizations;
- campaigning for improvements in disabled people's lives;
- providing information to support independence and equality for disabled
  people.

RADAR's website opens up communication within a network of 500 local
and national member organizations. It should also be a favourite site for
everyone with an interest in disability. Alongside the essential information
and publications on life as a disabled person, you will find regularly updated
news, information on important disability issues and links to other useful
sites.

References

Allport, G (1954) *The Nature of Prejudice*, Beacon Press, Boston

Beabout, G R and Wennemann, D J (1994) *Applied Professional Ethics*, University Press of America, Maryland

Boshear, W and Albrecht, K (1977) *Understanding People: Models and concepts*, University Associates, California

Bowden, J and Marton, F (1998) *The University of Learning: Beyond quality and competence in higher education*, Kogan Page, London

Bramley, P (1996) *Evaluating Training Effectiveness* (2nd edn), McGraw-Hill, London

Carmichael, S and Hamilton, C (1967) *Black Power: The politics of liberation in America*, Vintage, New York

Clark, K E and Miller, G A (eds) (1970) *Psychology: The behavioural and social science survey*, Prentice Hall, New Jersey

Clements, P (2000) *What Does Good Equal Opportunities Training Look Like?*, unpublished doctoral thesis, Brunel University, London

Commission for Racial Equality [Online] www.cre.gov.uk

Easterby-Smith, M (1994) *Evaluating Management Development, Training and Education* (2nd edn), Gower, London

Gidomal, R, Mahtani, D and Porter, D (2001) *The British and How to Deal with Them*, Middlesex University Press, London

Hamblin, A C (1974) *Evaluation and Control of Training*, McGraw-Hill, Maidenhead

Hill, W (1985) *Learning: A survey of psychological interpretations*, Harper and Row, London

HM Government (2000) *Modernizing Government*, White Paper (March), HMSO, London

HM Government Cabinet Office (1999) *Modernizing Government: A diverse civil service* [Online] www.cabinet-office.gov.uk/civil service/21st century

HM Government Cabinet Office (2002) [Online] www.cabinet-office.gov.uk/modern gov/whatismg.htm

Honey, P and Mumford, A (1986) *Using Your Learning Styles* (2nd edn), Peter Honey, Maidenhead

Kandola, R S *et al* (1991) *Equal Opportunities Can Damage Your Health!*, Pearn Kandola Downs, Oxford

Kearns, P (2000) *Maximising Your ROI in Training: Delivering measurable added value through employee development*, Financial Times Publications/Prentice Hall, London

Kirkpatrick, D L (1976) Evaluation of Training, in *Training and Development Handbook*, ed R L Craig, McGraw-Hill, London

Kirkpatrick, D L (1994) *Evaluating Training: The four levels*, Berrett-Koehler, San Francisco

Lippman, W (1922) *Public Opinion*, Free Press, New York

Local Government Association (2000) [Online] www.lga.gov.uk

Macpherson, W (1999) *The Stephen Lawrence Inquiry: Report of an inquiry by Sir William Macpherson of Cluny*, HMSO, London

Marton, F and Booth, S (1997) *Learning and Awareness*, Lawrence Erlbaum Associates, London

Mayo, A (2004) Making it All Add Up, *Personnel Today*, February

McKenzie, I (2000) Policing After Macpherson, *Police Journal*, **73** (4), pp 323–40

Munro, G D and Ditto, P H (1997) Biased assimilation, attitude polarization, and affect in reactions to stereotype-relevant scientific information, *Personality and Social Psychology Bulletin*, 23, pp 636–53

National Grid Transco (2002) [Online] www.investis.com/ngt/ara_2005/er_iiop.html

National Police Training (NPT) (2001) *Trainers Development Programme*, NPT, Office for Government Commerce

Neyroud, P and Beckley, A (2001) *Policing Ethics and Human Rights*, Willan, Collumpton

ODPM (2003) *Sustainable Communities: Building for the Future*, February, www.odpm.gov.uk

Patton, M Q (1978) *Utilization Focused Evaluation*, Sage, Thousand Oaks, Calif

Pawson, R and Tilley, N (1997) *Realistic Evaluation*, Sage, London

Phillips, J J (1995) Return on Investment: Beyond the four levels, in *Academy of HRD 1995 Conference Proceedings*, ed E Holton, 2–5 March, St Louis, Missouri

Phillips, J J (1996) Measuring ROI: the fifth level of evaluation, *Technical and Skills Training*, **3** (April), pp 10–13

Phillips, J J (1997) *Handbook of Training Evaluation and Measurement Methods* (3rd edn), Gulf, Houston

Prosser, M and Trigwell, K (1997) Towards an understanding of individual act of teaching and learning, in *Higher Education Research and Development*, vol 16, no. 2, pp 241–51

Race, P (2001) Evaluating Training Resources, *Training Journal* (November)

Reber, A S and Reber, I (2001) *The Penguin Dictionary of Psychology*, Penguin, Harmondsworth

Schön, D A (1983) *The Reflective Practitioner*, Basic Books, New York

Spinks, T and Clements, P (1993) *A Practical Guide to Facilitation Skills: A real-world approach*, Kogan Page, London

Thorpe, M (1988) *Evaluating Open and Distance Learning*, Open University Press, Milton Keynes

Tuckman, B W (1965) Developmental sequences in small groups, *Psychological Bulletin*, 63, pp 384–99

United Nations (2000) *United Nations Expert Group Meeting on Managing Diversity in the Civil Service*, [Online] www.un.org

Warr, P B, Bird, M and Rackham, N (1970) *The Evaluation of Management Training*, Gower, Aldershot

Index

NB: page numbers in *italic* indicate figures and tables